Presented To:

Jo Evelyn

From:

Date:

The JOY of intercession

OTHER BOOKS BY BENI JOHNSON

The Happy Intercessor

Beautiful One:
A Walk In Deeper Intimacy
with the One Who Created Us

Experiencing the Heavenly Realm (with Judy Franklin)

AVAILABLE FROM DESTINY IMAGE PUBLISHERS

A HAPPY *Intercessor* DEVOTIONAL

The JOY of intercession

A 40 Day ENCOUNTER

BENI JOHNSON

DESTINY IMAGE® PUBLISHERS, INC.

P.O. Box 310, Shippensburg, PA 17257-0310

"Promoting Inspired Lives."

This book and all other Destiny Image, Revival Press, Mercy Place, Fresh Bread, Destiny Image Fiction, and Treasure House books are available at Christian bookstores and distributors worldwide.

For a U.S. bookstore nearest you, call 1-800-722-6774.

For more information on foreign distributors, call 717-532-3040.

Or reach us on the Internet: www.destinyimage.com

Trade Paper ISBN: 978-0-7684-3882-6

Ebook ISBN: 978-0-7684-8963-7

For Worldwide Distribution, Printed in the U.S.A.

1 2 3 4 5 6 7 8 / 15 14 13 12 11

Dedication

I want to dedicate this book to you the reader. Thank you for taking the time to go through this book; for seeking after the heart of God; the longing to know His heartbeat; to feel Him in your everyday. We all have a place in us that longs for Him. As you read these pages and take time with Him, I know that He will meet you in a greater way and your life will be changed.

Acknowledgments

I thank my husband for being the greatest man alive. You are amazing! My life with you has been beyond my dreams. You have always let me be me, and you have always let me soar with Jesus. You have supported me in my book projects all the way, but most of all you have supported me in my life, this happy adventure. I love you with all my heart!

A huge thanks to all my wild, wonderful friends; we are crazy for Jesus. Thanks for your faithful prayer covering!

Endorsements

I love this book! It may be the best book on prayer ever. *The Happy Intercessor* is alive with Presence. Learn the secret of the secret place: how to capture the heartbeat of heaven and pray it into our world—but be happy while you're at it. The first opportunity I had to fellowship with Beni she invited me for a walk around her city. As we went over the now famous Sundial Bridge mentioned in Chapter 4 (where we find out how to "own your city") the thing that impacted me most was her joy. It was not noisy joy. And it felt like Heaven listened when she spoke. Beni seemed thoroughly at rest, confident in a *big* God, so aware of the world around, and so alive with the sense that when she prayed earth obeyed. I know now that she got that through her journey into God's heart. If you live it, you can give it away. That is what Beni does in this book. *The Happy Intercessor* is a gift for every person hungry to know God face to face. This book is a must for every person seeking significance. From classical theology with a down-to-earth prophetic twist to mastering the mystical realm, *The Happy Intercessor* is practical, pragmatic, and personal. Take this book and lay down in God…I think you'll find you're soaring!

Bonnie Chavda
Sr. Assoc. Pastor, All Nations Church
Cofounder, The Watch of the Lord
Charlotte, North Carolina

I have read no less than 40 books on intercession. Some challenged me to pray more, others helped me to see God's design for prayer, but few kept my rapt attention like Beni Johnson's *The Happy Intercessor*. This is one of the most interesting books on intercession I have ever read. Beni has the unique ability to blend the heavenly with the practical through her own life stories and biblical insight. This is a must read for every person called to intercession, especially if you are having trouble being consistent at it.

John Paul Jackson
Founder, Streams Ministries International
Author, *Unmasking the Jezebel Spirit*

I have known Beni Johnson for more than 30 years. I have watched her relationship with God grow into one of the most beautiful love stories that has ever been told. Just spending a few minutes with her will cause you to hunger for more intimacy with the Father and will remind you of your first love. *The Happy Intercessor* is more than a good book on prayer; it is a Holy Spirit journey into the very heart of the Father. This book could revolutionize the way you relate to God on every level. Let the journey begin!

Kris Vallotton
Cofounder, Bethel School of Supernatural Ministry
Author, *The Supernatural Ways of Royalty* and
Developing a Supernatural Lifestyle

This is a book that makes intercession engaging, exciting, and dare I say…exhilarating? I think it can spark a revolution among people like me who need fresh, innovative insight into how to pray "without ceasing" and still be energized. With this book in hand, we can recruit an army of "killer sheep" to police the heavens in every community and the top of every mountain of influence…and enjoy the battle!

Lance Wallnau
Founder, Lance Learning Group

The Happy Intercessor is a one-of-a-kind manuscript, providing valuable insight into the often misunderstood realm of intercession. Like its author, this extraordinary book is real, down to earth, and refreshingly honest. *The Happy Intercessor* skillfully captures the true heart of intercession in a way that is uncomplicated, yet powerful in application.

Larry Randolph
Founder, Larry Randolph Ministries
Author, *Spirit Talk*, *The Coming Shift*
and *User Friendly Prophecy*

Contents

Foreword

Writing an endorsement or a foreword for a book is a great honor. This is especially true when you know the author and have seen how the message she has written has been lived out in her life. That being the case, I've never been more honored to write on behalf of another author than I have with this one: my wife.

Anytime I introduce Beni in my travels or present her teaching CDs, I mention that she is a sign and a wonder—*she is a happy intercessor*. That comment usually gets a laugh because it is one area of church life where harshness, intolerance, and depression have been considered the price of admission. That nervous laughter also reveals a hope that it could be different. We have discovered as a church that it can and must be different.

I was there when the prophetic declaration was made over her life about becoming an intercessor. We both had been exposed to intercessors who made us want anything but that calling in life. Their *burden*, which we discovered later was just a fancy word for depression, was not a very inviting image for those of us who were truly wanting to learn how to pray. But she knew enough not to reject the word.

I remember the night my wife was changed from timid to bold—from a *behind the scenes* kind of person to being in front, giving direction. It happened in one night. She had an encounter with the Lord in Toronto in which she shook like a dishrag. It was fearful and amazing to watch. All fear of man and intimidation seemed to be shaken right out of her. A lioness was born that night.

Her journey in intercession began the best way possible. She was a lover of God first and foremost. And that became the context for all her learning. Sometimes you just don't know the keys and profound principles for bringing a breakthrough in an area, but you can always take time to love God. That is her story. While Beni's insights and experiences are true and profound, they were not learned because of a desire to be powerful. They are all born out of the desire just to know and love God with every possible breath. I believe that to be the secret to effective prayer—to love God, period. Because loving God develops a partnership. And it's much more fun to pray with God than merely to pray to Him.

I pray this devotional will bring you to an even deeper walk and joyous life with your heavenly Father—the journey is about to begin!

Bill Johnson

Introduction

This devotional journal is a continuation of the concepts and principles presented in *The Happy Intercessor*. It is designed to help you discover the intercessor in you.

Each day is divided into four inspiring and thought-provoking sections:

- Scripture—relevant and life-changing words from God.

- Devotion—excerpts from *The Happy Intercessor*.

- Reflections—questions and ideas for meaningful pause.

- Meditative Action—excerpts from *The Happy Intercessor* and thoughts that prompt introspection and provoke activity.

Each day brings you closer to discovering God's love and plan for your life. You will experience for yourself through personal devotion and journaling how to be directly involved in intercessory prayer for His children next door—and worldwide.

Q&A—PRAYER AND INTERCESSION

The following questions and answers give you a basis on which to build your time in devotion with God and a springboard for your time of journaling. I present these to you as a way of connecting with the joy of intercessory prayer.

Q. The Bible doesn't mention an official position of an intercessor. From where did today's Christians get this?

A. Even though the Bible doesn't have an official title for an intercessor, there are many biblical examples of times when God looked for an intercessor.

In Isaiah 59:16 it says, *"He saw that there was no man, and wondered that there was no intercessor; therefore His own arm brought salvation for Him; and His own righteousness, it sustained Him."* Then again in Ezekiel 22:30, *"So I sought for a man among them who would make a wall, and stand in the gap before Me on behalf of the land, that I should not destroy it; but I found no one."*

Many people, especially the prophets in the Bible, defined *intercessor* for us through their lives, even though they were not given that title. One of those would be Moses. Moses stood before God on many occasions to ask God for mercy on behalf of a stiff-necked people. On one occasion, God told Moses that He would change His mind because of him (see Num. 14:20).

God looks for those who will stand in the gap for whatever the reason. Another thing demonstrated in these verses is that God really does want us to partner with Him for His Kingdom to be realized on earth as it is in Heaven.

Q. What is the difference between prayer and intercession?

A. *Prayer* in the Old Testament is, for the most part, the same word as *intercession*. In the New Testament, the word *prayer* means to worship, to petition, or make a request. The definition of the word *intercession*, in the New Testament, is very similar to *prayer:*

The word *paga*, translated intercession in the Old Testament, means "by accident or violence, cause to entreat, fall, light upon, meet together."

There is not much difference between the two, except for the violent (*paga*) part of intercession. That would involve a more intense part of prayer.

I believe that intercession is the action of pleading on somebody's behalf, the action of attempting to settle a dispute or a prayer to God, a god, or a saint on behalf of somebody or something.

To intercede is to plead with somebody in authority on behalf of somebody else, especially somebody who is to be punished for something. It is to speak in support of somebody involved in a dispute; it is an attempt to settle a dispute between others.

Intercession involves reaching God, meeting God, and entreating Him for His favor.

Q. Are we all called to pray and intercede?

A. Yes, we are. We are all called to have a relationship with our Father. And out of that, it should be automatic for us to pray. But I do believe that a person can have a *gift* of intercession—a gift given by God. You can tell that you have this gift if all that you want to do is be with God and if you feel yourself being pulled into prayer by what you see around you.

Q. Why pray?

A. Remember, prayer is talking to God. I love being around my husband. We have a wonderful relationship. We spend time together and talk and share our lives. I feel that God is looking for those who will commune (talk) with Him and be with Him. He is our Father and does want to share His heart with us. As He shares, we in response will want to pray. It is a partnering.

Rejoice always, pray without ceasing, in everything give thanks; for this is the will of God in Christ Jesus for you (1 Thessalonians 5:16-18).

The Bible tells us that praying and giving thanks is God's will for our lives.

Q. How long does someone have to pray for a particular issue?

A. From my own experience, I believe that there are life assignments that God gives each of us. For me, that is praying for the fivefold government of the Church to be set up and in working order. But, I also think that God gives us short-term prayer assignments. How do you know when that assignment is over? You will feel a lifting or release from the assignment.

There are also times when an assignment will come and go. For example, for several years I had been praying for a particular region and even for a specific leader in that region. Then, it all stopped for a year. One morning I woke up and thought, *I wonder how that person is doing?* The desire to pray for this region and person all came back, and I began to pray again. I think the key here is to be sensitive to His voice, and you will know.

Q. How do we know that we are praying to God's will?

A. To be honest there are times when we hit and miss, and from that, we learn how to know. We always must use the Bible as the guideline as well.

"In the same way the Spirit also helps our weakness; for we do not know how to pray as we should, but the Spirit Himself intercedes for us with groanings too deep for words" (Rom. 8:26 NASB). The spirit in a person knows the person, so with the Holy Spirit. He knows the Father. So if we are tapped into the Holy Spirit, we will have a much higher percentage of our prayers being right on track.

We need to be careful that we are not manipulating with our prayers. I have addressed this issue in the devotional.

Q. When should we travail in prayer?

A. For me, travailing is not something I choose. It chooses me.

Q. What about praying in the Spirit; how does praying in tongues become intercession?

A. For an intercessor, tongues play an important role as we pray. I spend a lot of time praying in tongues. I like to use my prayer language when I take walks. As I walk, I begin praying in tongues, and I can feel my spirit begin to engage with the Holy Spirit. As I continue to pray, things will come to my mind, and I will speak in tongues over those things. It can become easy to pray yet not engage with the Holy Spirit. It can become just something we do with no life in it. But engaging with our spirit language causes our prayers to become effective.

I had a friend come to me and ask for prayer. As I began praying for her, I felt like I was to speak into her ear and pray in tongues. As I began praying in tongues over her, both of us felt our spirits engaging with the tongue. She was able to receive and get breakthrough in what she was going through.

Q. Intercession and decrees. What is a decree?

A. I believe that there are two ways to pray. One is petition, which is making a request; and the other is the declaration, which comes from a place of faith or belief that it will be done. I feel that many intercessors are really good at petitioning, but that they don't know how to move into a place of faith, knowing that it is time to declare a thing as done.

Several years ago, I felt like it was time for us to begin to make declarations and to stop petitioning so much in our prayers. Our focus needed to shift from the posture of making requests before God to a posture of faith and taking the authority that is ours. I actually felt that there was a shift in our authority level. Because we had petitioned for so long, it was a time for us to begin declaring things into being.

When we take teams out to pray, I will tell them, "I want you to make a declaration or decree over this land." It would be similar to giving a prophetic word. You are using your words of declaration to cause a change.

Q. What are some tips for praying or using this devotional in a group?

A. When you call people together, you are going to have all different kinds of prayers. Some will be ready to violently go after God, and others will want to quietly pray, while others may want to have a list of things to pray over. As a leader, you need to set some ground rules. For example, when praying for a topic, you want to make sure that you exhaust the subject in praying before you go on to another. In many meetings, when someone starts out praying for something and then the next person moves on to something different, you haven't exhausted the prayer. There may be more that someone else wanted to pray. You want to make sure that everyone prays and completes the prayer before moving on to another topic.

Tell people in the group that they need to give everyone a chance to pray and that one or two people should not take over the prayer meeting.

I have found that the best way to bring a whole group together in prayer is to have them all soak in God's presence first. This brings everyone into the heart of God, and after soaking, you will find the prayer time to be much more rewarding and effective.

ENDNOTE

1. *New American Standard Exhaustive Concordance of the Bible, Hebrew-Aramaic and Greek Dictionary*, Robert L. Thomas, Ed., version 2.2, s.v. "Paga."

DAY 1

Unburden Yourself

*For this reason we also, from the day we heard of it, have **not ceased to pray** and make [special] request for you, [asking] that you may be filled with the full (deep and clear) knowledge of His will in all spiritual wisdom [in comprehensive insight into the ways and purposes of God] and in understanding and **discernment of spiritual things*** (Colossians 1:9 AMP).

DEVOTION

For many years, I didn't know that I was an intercessor. When I look back now, I can see all the signs: I spent so much time carrying so many feelings inside of me and internalizing them as if they were my own. For example, I would often walk into a room filled with people and start feeling and hearing their thoughts—thoughts which were often very negative.

Not realizing, however, that all of those feelings that I was experiencing were the gift that the Bible calls "discernment of spirits," I would carry those burdensome emotions as my own instead of releasing them in prayer. As a result, I became depressed. I became a "quiet one."

As a child I was told that I was shy. My parents didn't do this, but others did. Unfortunately, because so many people told me that I was shy, over and over, I began to think that I was shy. I took those words as truth. I agreed with those words and received them as my identity. Sadly, being shy eventually became a stronghold in my life that controlled me.

Going to my mom to pray gave me release from these things. When I prayed, it would help me release my feelings and give them to God.

(*The Happy Intercessor*, Chapter 1)

REFLECTIONS

1. Do you spend too much time internalizing others' feelings as if they were your own? *maybe*

2. Have you been labeled "shy"? Have you become "a quiet one" because you have believed what others have said about you? *Don't think so*

3. Is it common for you to hear or feel the thoughts or attitudes of others? How do you handle these often burdensome emotions? *Yes mull them over - then try to get distracted as they bring me down*

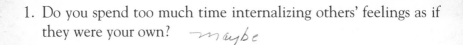

4. Is there a stronghold in your life that is controlling your happiness and your decision-making? *Not sure*

5. Write your definition of an intercessor. Are you an intercessor? *Someone who has strong burden for another + spends time + energy pleading before God for that person*

MEDITATIVE ACTION

In my teen years, I was still caught in this place of feeling a lot of feelings that were not my own. The problem was that I had stopped praying. I forgot what to do with all those feelings, so I carried them as mine. That led to a lot of depression in my earlier years.

Gratefully, when I turned 16, I had an encounter with God that changed my life. For the two years before the encounter, I had pretty much led my own life and done my own thing, and it brought me to a place of desperation. One night in church, there was a call to come forward to give your life to God, and I did, and I let it all out. I remember going before the Lord that night, crying out to Him and saying to the Lord, "All I want is you." I remember asking the Lord to take my life that night. And He did.

(*The Happy Intercessor*, Chapter 1)

If you are depressed or living in a place of desperation, give your life to God.

Are you willing to "let it all out" and ask God for more of Him in your life? Yes

DAY 2

All Things for Good

All things work together for good to those who love God, to those who are the called according to His purpose (Romans 8:28).

DEVOTION

When I was 17, I went to a discipleship training center for nine months. One of my roommates had a lot of mental instability. I was so concerned for her because I would feel what she was going through, but I did not make a connection that I was actually personally experiencing the same exact things that she was experiencing.

I remember being in the room one day with her, and we were both sitting on our beds. Such incredible despair overcame me that I remember feeling as though I wanted to give up on life. I didn't realize, however, that I was actually picking up the mental torment that my roommate was experiencing—feelings that I too had once experienced. I did not know what to do with these tormenting emotions! It did not click, and I had no idea that God was showing me that I was supposed to be praying for her.

Years later, as I began working in ministry, I would realize that God allowed the experiences of my past to show me the *purpose* for which He has truly called me to be used today.

(*The Happy Intercessor*, Chapter 1)

REFLECTIONS

1. Have you ever actually personally experienced the same exact things that someone else was experiencing? *I think so*

2. Are you so empathetic that you have a hard time distinguishing between your feelings and others' emotions? *Yes*

3. How hard is it for you to separate your feelings from those of a close friend or family member? *Extremely hard*

4. What do you do with tormenting emotions that you know are not your own? *Pray* *Try to run from*

5. Have you acknowledged your gift of empathy and used it to serve God's family? *No*

MEDITATIVE ACTION

I had a prayer life, but it was just a general prayer life. I prayed for my kids and my family or things that were going on in the church. I prayed because I thought that was what I was supposed to do. I did not pray out of relationship with the Holy Spirit.

(*The Happy Intercessor*, Chapter 1)

What could be your first step to learning how to pray out of a relationship with the Holy Spirit?

I don't know

Are you ready to take that first step? Why or why not?

I think so
I'm desperate

DAY 3

Life Renewed

Create in me a clean heart, O God, and renew a steadfast spirit within me (Psalm 51:10).

DEVOTION

For the most part, when we lived in Weaverville, CA, I spent my time as a mother of young children. For me, finding time to pray was extremely difficult. I remember that my prayer time was usually +doing the dishes, or else I had to wake up very early to read my Bible and pray. To be honest, it felt like more of an obligation than a desire. There was still something deep within me that truly desired to be with God, but because of my busy schedule, I would never really take the time to pursue that deep calling to deep. Looking back, I can see now that there was a pull to go deeper with God, but I did not know where to go or how to get there. And then renewal came.

In 1995, renewal came to our church in Weaverville. It was a time of great refreshing and joy. It was also a time when the Holy Spirit stirred up my heart, releasing me to be who I am. A brand-new season was coming. In this time of stirring, I felt Him speak to me a word that would change my life. I heard these words, "I want you to carry joy and intercession." My first thought was, "Is that possible?" I still only saw intercession as a depressed way of living.

(*The Happy Intercessor*, Chapter 1)

REFLECTIONS

1. Honestly, does reading the Bible and praying sometimes feel more like an obligation than a desire?

   Bible reading — No
   Praying — Yes

2. Do you feel a pull to go deeper with God, but don't know where to go or how to get there?   *Yes!*

3. Do you have a deep desire to be with God, but because of your busy schedule, you don't take the time to pursue that deep calling to deep?   *Yes - but schedule Not so busy Now Just don't know how to get there*

4. Do you think that a life of intercession would be depressing?

   No

5. When is the last time you have felt refreshed and joyful in your relationship with the Lord?   *Frequently - Especially during Bethel worship*

MEDITATIVE ACTION

With renewal, people were experiencing so much freedom. I had two different experiences during that time that I would call life-changing encounters with God. One of those experiences happened in Toronto, at John and Carol Arnott's church, Toronto Airport Christian Fellowship (TACF). My parents, my husband, and I were attending a conference there on the Father's Blessing, which was the pulse of the whole outpouring there at TACF. After one of the meetings, Bill and I walked to the back of the room where there were people everywhere on the floor, much laughter, and Holy Spirit drunkenness. Acts 2:15 says, *"For these are not drunk, as you suppose, since it is only the third hour of the day."* When the Holy Spirit's power hit the disciples in the upper room, they looked and acted like they were drunk.

(*The Happy Intercessor*, Chapter 1)

Are you willing to get "drunk" in the Holy Spirit?

Yes!

Write what you think that experience would be like.

I'm a little Nervous + holding back
But

Freeing

DAY 4

For Pulling Down Strongholds

For the weapons of our warfare are not carnal but mighty in God for pulling down strongholds (2 Corinthians 10:4).

DEVOTION

Have you ever noticed that drunken people don't care what other people think about what they are doing at that moment? Well, there was such a man at that meeting that night. We noticed him staggering around the back, laying his hands on people. As he did, they would fall to the ground. God was using that man as a Holy Spirit conduit. Some would laugh with Holy Spirit laughter; others would shake under the power of the Holy Spirit.

The next day, we went back to the morning session. As the speaker began speaking something about the Father's love, I felt the presence of God and began to cry. I asked the Lord what had gone on the night before. "What was that all about?" I heard these words: "I was shaking out of you the strongholds of your life and birthing who you are." From that day on, the fear that had guided my life left. The stronghold had been broken. I became a different person through that unusual encounter with God.

(*The Happy Intercessor*, Chapter 1)

REFLECTIONS

1. Do you care too much about what other people think about you? About what you say, wear, eat, believe…?

   Yes

2. Have you ever witnessed God using someone as a Holy Spirit conduit? What was your first reaction?

   Yes   skeptical - critical - envious

3. When was the last time you felt the presence of God? What was He telling you? *Daily - Come closer*

   Rejoice
   STOP TV - @ least for Now

4. How many strongholds in your life can you easily identify? How many can God and you destroy together?

   T.V.   All

5. What fear is guiding your life? *- unbelief of Anne*

   Financial worries
   Ageing

MEDITATIVE ACTION

Now, I have to tell you that the devil doesn't just sit back and say, "Oh, I can't tempt her anymore." No, he tries to come and get me to make agreement with him. The devil wants us to agree with our old life-style patterns. Once we agree with him, he has control again. The devil will allow a familiar spirit to come to us and get us to go back to thinking old ways, but born-again believers are equipped with a supernatural strength to say, "No."

So when a familiar spirit, such as self pity, comes and tries to get us to agree and say, "Yes, that's the way I am," we can now say (because the stronghold has been removed), "No, that is not who I am anymore." I felt as though God had given me a power tool for my life and the strength to use it against the lies from the devil.

(*The Happy Intercessor*, Chapter 1)

How can you stop the devil from tricking you into returning to your old lifestyle?

Agree w/ him in his temptations

Name three things that you can do to keep from thinking about the old ways and start saying "No."

1. *Be alert - watch for his temptations*
2. *Shout NO to his lies*
3. *Refuse to listen to him & agree w/ God's word re your victory & who you are*

DAY 5

Day by Day

Therefore we do not lose heart. Even though our outward man is perishing, yet the inward man is being renewed day by day (2 Corinthians 4:16).

DEVOTION

At this point, my prayer life really began to change. My prayer life was not so much about asking for things anymore but just about wanting to be with the Lord. And I would just worship Him for an hour or more at a time. Music played a vital part in the personal renewal of my life. I am able to tap into His presence through the tool of worship music. So I would put a worship CD on, sit in God's presence, and enjoy Him. His presence was deep inside of me, in my spirit.

Around that time, Bethel began to move into renewal. It actually happened one night when my husband called people down who wanted to be renewed and refreshed. Many people came forward, and we began praying for them. We went over to pray for one lady, and all I can say is that God apprehended this woman in that moment. Bill and I looked at each other and said, "There it is." We knew that renewal had come to Bethel and that the church would never be the same. I looked at the woman's husband and told him, "She will never be the same." Looking back, she has never been the same, and neither has the church.

(*The Happy Intercessor*, Chapter 1)

REFLECTIONS

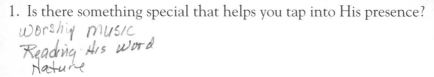

1. Is there something special that helps you tap into His presence?

   worship music
   Reading His Word
   Nature

2. Do you want to be renewed and refreshed? In what ways?

   Oh yes, so much!
   More constant love for everyone - patience, longsuffering
   Carry His Presence always

3. Have you gone forward in a church service expecting something extraordinary to happen, but it seemed as if nothing did happen?

   Not so much

4. Has your church gone through a season of refreshing? Why or why not?

   Not settled on a church right now

5. Is it scary or exciting to think that you will "never be the same"?

   Exciting

MEDITATIVE ACTION

After their experience with God, the church members would be completely different. Their lives would be completely changed; there would be more freedom, both emotionally and physically. I remember one night walking up to a young lady who was waiting for prayer, and I found out that she was a missionary who had been on the mission field for two years. She had just come home and was absolutely exhausted and burned out from ministry.

I began to pray for her, and she fell on the floor under the power of God. For an hour I sat with her on the floor and watched God completely, radically change her life. She laughed; she cried. I laughed; I cried. We laughed and cried together. After an hour, she got up completely different, a brand-new person. She no longer had the exhaustion or the depression. She still lives out of that place of freedom today.

(*The Happy Intercessor*, Chapter 1)

If you feel exhausted, depressed, or burned out from ministry, family obligations, and/or career challenges, pray now for emotional and physical renewal.

Give God the go-ahead to radically change your life—do it now.

DAY 6

Experiencing His Love

But do not let this one fact escape your notice, beloved, that with the Lord one day is like a thousand years, and a thousand years like one day (2 Peter 3:8 NASB).

DEVOTION

One of my favorite things that happened during that time was that God began bringing so many of us into that deep, intimate place where we could truly experience His love. At times, many of us felt like His presence was so heavy on us and in us that we would never come out of it. I remember a friend calling me one day and asking me if I would pray for her. She was in His presence, in that deep, faraway place, and she needed to be released so that she could cook dinner for her family.

This depth of His presence was new for many. What we learned was that we were moving into true intercession. There was a mixture of love, joy, and extreme heartbreak. This heartbreak that we would feel was from the extreme, intense love that our Father has for His children worldwide. Like in the story of the prodigal son, we felt the Father missing His children and longing for them to come back to Him and His love. And we found that when we would let ourselves experience the longing of a heavenly Father, who was desperate to pour His love upon us, that we could almost become "addicted" to His glorious presence.

(*The Happy Intercessor*, Chapter 2).

REFLECTIONS

1. Have you ever felt like God's presence was so heavy on you and in you that you would never come out of it? If yes, write what you experienced. If no, write what you think it would be like.

   No -
   Like coming home

2. What does it mean to you to be "moving into true intercession"?

   Feeling the heartbeat of God

3. Does it break your heart that there are so many people world-wide who don't know the Father's love?

   Yes

4. What is keeping you from becoming addicted to God's presence?

   Laziness? Anxiety

5. Why do you think God is "desperate" to pour out His love on His children?

   Because of His heart of love

MEDITATIVE ACTION

Oftentimes I *see* faces, places, and situations in my mind's eye. I often feel as if God is showing me things that I need to think about and *brood over* in the way that a mother hen broods over her eggs. Genesis 1:1 says, *"Earth was a soup of nothingness, a bottomless emptiness, an inky blackness. God's Spirit brooded like a bird above the watery abyss"* (TM). To be honest, most of the time when I am in this place, I just agree. I agree with the plans that God already has for people's lives, for regions, and for the earth. "Yes God, do that God…go there, Father…that's amazing, Lord Jesus." When I pray this way, I feel as though I am praying from His heart and calling into existence the very desires that are already in the heart of God.

We carry the life of the Kingdom within us (see Luke 17:21). It will flow out of us in our intercessions.

(*The Happy Intercessor*, Chapter 2)

Have you taken steps to learn about your community, state, region, and the world regarding sharing the gospel and providing for the needs of His children?

Are you "agreeing" with God when you pray?

DAY 7

No Agenda Required

Whatever God has promised gets stamped with the Yes of Jesus. In Him, this is what we preach and pray, the great Amen, God's Yes and our Yes together, gloriously evident (2 Corinthians 1:20 TM).

DEVOTION

When we go into God's presence, and tap into the realm of Heaven, we position ourselves to receive great breakthrough. One of the things that we need to be careful about is going before God with our *own* agendas. Sometimes I think we go before God and already have an idea of what we want God to do; so we close ourselves off from receiving from and partnering with God and what He may want to do in the moment. In fact, God may want to do something completely different. It is almost as if we say, "Here God, here is my idea; now do it my way." When we do that, we handcuff God. We are no longer partnering with Him.

Often, when people ask me to pray for them, they come with an agenda—or an idea—of what they want to ask God to do. When I am praying for people and I ask them what they need prayer for, sometimes their requests are not what is on God's agenda for the moment. We need to learn how to be sensitive and move with the Holy Spirit. We need to listen to the heartbeat of God and not always present our ideas to Him. It's not about whether agendas are wrong or right, but when I just want to spend time with God and feel His presence, I don't bring any agenda.

(*The Happy Intercessor*, Chapter 2)

REFLECTIONS

1. Have you tapped into the realm of Heaven and positioned yourself to receive great breakthrough?

2. Have you closed yourself off from receiving from and partnering with God because you have your own agenda?

3. Can you accept the fact that sometimes your requests are not what are on God's agenda for the moment?

4. How sensitive are you to the move of the Holy Spirit and hearing the heartbeat of God?

5. When you want to spend time with God and feel His presence, remember—don't bring an agenda of your own.

MEDITATIVE ACTION

I woke up praying for one of our sons, Brian. I prayed for his safety. Right after I prayed, we got a call from him in the middle of the night telling us that he was driving home from a trip down south. He had fallen asleep at the wheel while driving and had run off the road. He called to tell us that he was OK. I was so thankful that I had been woken up to pray.

Intercession is just the fruit of being with Him. It was birthed in my own heart because of spending time with Him. I go into His presence to love Him, to experience "Spirit-to-spirit"—His Spirit with my spirit. When I experienced this for the first time, I remember just being with Him and feeling our hearts connecting. It felt like my heart was picking up the same heartbeat as His—pouring upon me "liquid love" from His heart. His heart was broken for humanity. Our two hearts are intertwined. When you feel that, when you see His heart broken and His amazing love, your only response can be to pray with burning passion— with compassion for a lost generation.

(*The Happy Intercessor*, Chapter 2).

Go into His presence and experience Him Spirit-to-spirit.

Pray with burning passion for those who don't know Him or have rejected Him.

DAY 8

Yes!

But God told him "It was good that you wanted to build a Temple in my honor—most commendable!" (1 Kings 8:18 TM).

DEVOTION

God's *yes* together with our *yes* is what brings about breakthrough in prayer. I'm continually amazed that God would choose to partner with us. But, at the same time, it makes all the sense in the world that He would want us to join with Him in making history. We are, after all, His children. He is a great and all-powerful God and also a loving and caring Father who, I believe, wants to be involved in our lives. Incredibly, He also wants us to be involved in His Kingdom. He wants us to help build His Kingdom here on earth. Some of the prophetic acts that we do come from the Lord, but I think that some of the things that we do are good ideas that the Father says, "Yeah, that's good."

First Kings chapter 8 says that God chose David and that it was in David's heart to build a house for the Lord (see 1 Kings 8:16-17). God told David in verse 18, *"David…you did well that it was in your heart"* (1 Kings 8:18). Wow! That is our God. God chose a man whom He knew would say, "Yes!" And God said, "Yes" to David, and everything else is history. God's *yes* to you and your *yes* to Him are all that is needed.

(*The Happy Intercessor*, Chapter 2)

REFLECTIONS

1. Do you want to join with God in making history?

2. Do you want God to be involved in your life?

3. Do you want to build God's Kingdom on earth as it is in Heaven?

4. Do you want to say "Yes" when God brings a good idea to your mind?

5. Do you want to follow through on God's good idea?

MEDITATIVE ACTION

When God gives us strategies to pray—you know, the ones that we burn with—we can become so focused on His voice that we don't become distracted. Nothing can take us away from His voice. There were times during delivery of her own child that my daughter and I would lock eyes as well. It was how she got through the intense times. She drew strength from looking into my eyes. There was an intensity or determination in my eyes that she picked up on, which kept her going.

There are times in our lives when we must stay closer, locking onto His words and His vision. God gives us prayer strategies, and we look to Him for focus and understanding on how to pray with results. Then the birthing will come.

(*The Happy Intercessor*, Chapter 2).

Focus on God so intently that you block out all distractions.

Lock onto God's words and vision so that your prayers will yield results.

DAY 9

An Offensive Lifestyle

As a result, we are no longer to be children, tossed here and there by waves and carried about by every wind of doctrine, by the trickery of men, by craftiness in deceitful scheming (Ephesians 4:14 NASB).

DEVOTION

For intercessors, it is extremely important to understand that God has already given us the ball. We are the offensive team. If you don't understand that, if you are not praying from a place of victory, then you will be an intercessor whose prayer life is marked with defeat. You will be one who is always trying to protect what God has given you from the devil's plans or, worse yet, running after the devil and trying to figure out what he is doing. How wrong is that? If you do not understand that God has already given you the ball, you will live in fear and pray from a place of lack.

A good player will be so focused on his target that it feels like there is no one else around. A good player does not just throw the ball around. Similarly, we can't just throw our prayers around here and there.

(*The Happy Intercessor*, Chapter 3)

REFLECTIONS

1. You have the ball, and are on the offensive team. Are you ready to win?

2. Are you praying from a place of victory? If not, then you are an intercessor whose prayer life is marked with defeat.

3. Are you living in fear and praying from a place of lack?

4. Are you a good player who is so focused on your target that it feels like there is no one else around?

5. Are you throwing your prayers around here and there, or are you focused on God's will and good pleasure?

MEDITATIVE ACTION

Offensive teams call the plays. They must have confidence that they are going to win. They have to believe that they will win because they know that they control the ball. The devil lost the ball at Calvary.

As an intercessor, your job is to find out what God wants to do, which is the opposite of what the enemy is saying. Then you begin to pray what God wants. You don't allow the enemy to bring distraction. You have to make a choice not to partner with fear.

This is how intercessors live an offensive lifestyle. They pray according to God's plans, and they pray from a place of victory.

(*The Happy Intercessor*, Chapter 3)

Call some winning plays today—defeat the devil in all his strategies!

Do not partner with fear—live an offensive lifestyle by always praying from a place of victory!

DAY 10

No Fear Zone

Do not be afraid of sudden fear, nor of the onslaught of the wicked when it comes; for the Lord will be your confidence and will keep your foot from being caught (Proverbs 3:25-26 NASB).

DEVOTION

Fear has a way of coming up and biting you. Everything seems to be going great in your life and you are walking in peace. All of a sudden, there fear is, trying to envelope you, trying to destroy your peace. We as believers have to make a choice to resist fear. We as a family had to make a choice that we would not partner with fear. The devil has legal rights only if we agree with him. The tool he uses to get us is fear. He does not play fair with us. He will go right for our soft spots.

Do you ever just sit back and think about the world, what it looks like now, and what is really going on? Why are things in world events happening? What is really making those events happen? What is the root? Not just on the surface, but deeper—what is making things go the way they are going?

(*The Happy Intercessor,* Chapter 3)

REFLECTIONS

1. Do you ever just sit back and think about the world, what it looks like now, and what is really going on?

2. Why are things in world events happening?

3. What is really making those events happen?

4. What is the root?

5. Not just on the surface, but deeper—what is making things go the way they are going?

MEDITATIVE ACTION

When I look at the world, I can recognize the devil's plan. The root is fear. It really is a simple plan. All the devil has to do is make sure that we walk in fear; then all of our responses will be out of that place of fear. The most repeated command in the Bible is "Do not fear." From Genesis to Revelation, God has repeatedly told us not to fear. God knows our humanness.

When I sit back and look at the world and see what God is doing, it makes me happy. Do these words sound familiar? *"For I know the thoughts that I think toward you, says the Lord, thoughts of peace and not of evil, to give you a future and a hope"* (Jer. 29:11).

(*The Happy Intercessor*, Chapter 3)

Choose today not to be fearful and to rely on God's faithfulness to overcome your challenges.

Write down five thoughts that you believe the Lord is thinking toward you.

1

2

3

4

5

DAY 11

Hit the Mark

When the Lord brought back the captivity of Zion, We were like those who dream. Then our mouth was filled with laughter, And our tongue with singing. Then they said among the nations, "The Lord has done great things for them." The Lord has done great things for us, And we are glad. Bring back our captivity, O Lord, As the streams in the South. Those who sow in tears Shall reap in joy. He who continually goes forth weeping, Bearing seed for sowing, Shall doubtless come again with rejoicing, Bringing his sheaves with him (Psalm 126).

DEVOTION

As intercessors, we need to be focused in our prayers and our strategies. Effective intercessors know how to listen for the plays that God calls, and they know how to catch the ball and make the touchdown. Effective intercessors are offensive intercessors; they know how to hit the mark.

One of the meanings for intercession is to "strike the mark." This phrase derives from the Hebrew word, *paga*.[1] *Paga* means "to meet"; it is the violent part of intercession. Job 36:32 tells of a violent *paga* meeting: *"He covers His hands with lightning and commands it to strike [the mark]."*

If we are going to be a people who pray with an offensive purpose, "hitting the mark" in our prayers, we must be on a quest to search the heart of God. How can we do that? Where do we go to find God's heart? We go to His Word to find His heart. I find it interesting that the word *Torah* comes from the root word *yarah*, which means "to shoot straight," or "to hit the mark."[2] God has given us the Bible to show us His heart.

(*The Happy Intercessor*, Chapter 3)

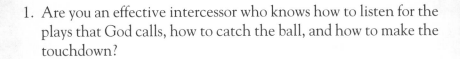

REFLECTIONS

1. Are you an effective intercessor who knows how to listen for the plays that God calls, how to catch the ball, and how to make the touchdown?

2. Are you an offensive intercessor who knows how to hit the mark?

3. How diligently have you been searching to know God's heart?

4. Have you followed the trail to God's heart that is described in the Bible?

5. What do you like best about searching the Bible for truths? The least?

MEDITATIVE ACTION

In the late 1990s, there was a real push for people to pray directly from the Scriptures. Praying the Scriptures is a great way to pray the heart of God. It's all there in writing, just waiting for us to pray and proclaim it. One of the main things that I learned during that season was how to meditate on the Scriptures.

I learned how to take a chapter or a small section of Scripture and begin to think or meditate on it. I would read the verses over and over slowly. As I did, they began to go into my spirit. The Scriptures would become alive in my spirit and mind. Then, I would find myself praying from those verses. I would find new meaning and new revelation in each verse. My prayers would come alive.

(*The Happy Intercessor*, Chapter 3)

Pray for 30 minutes from the Scriptures.

Write your prayer from one of the Psalms.

ENDNOTES

1. Dutch Sheets, *Intercessory Prayer* (Ventura, CA: Regal Books, 1996), 50.

2. Allan Moorhead, "Law Verses Grace, Part 1" (2003), http://mayimhayim.org/Allen/Law%20vs%20Grace%201.htm; accessed Sept. 17, 2008.

DAY 12

Revealed Through His Spirit

And my speech and my preaching were not with persuasive words of human wisdom, but in demonstration of the Spirit and of power, that your faith should not be in the wisdom of men but in the power of God (1 Corinthians 2:4-5).

DEVOTION

Apostle Paul was a very learned man and was more than able to use persuasive words of human wisdom to make his point. Instead, he chose to come in the Holy Spirit's power. Paul then went on to say that we don't even know the good things that God has prepared for those who love Him.

In First Corinthians 2:9-10, Paul tells us that we can know the things of God because God has revealed them to us through His Spirit. Paul tells us that the Spirit is searching deeply into the heart of God. No one knows the heart of God except the Spirit. This is where it gets exciting. What we see in these Scriptures is that God is telling us that He has given us the ability to know the things of God. If we dive into the Spirit of God, we can know what is in the heart of God. Wow! God wants us to know Him and to know His ways.

(*The Happy Intercessor*, Chapter 3)

REFLECTIONS

1. How adept are you at using persuasive words of human wisdom to make your point?

   Not so good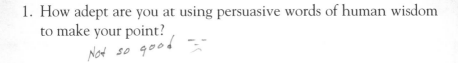

2. Why do you think that we don't know all the good things that God has prepared for those who love Him?

   Haven't put self in position to learn?

3. Has God revealed things to you through His Spirit?

   Yes

4. If you dive into the Spirit of God, can you know what is in the heart of God? *Oh Yes — I am told so*

5. How eager are you to know God and His ways?

   I feel eager — Need more discipline

MEDITATIVE ACTION

One of the targets that we have in our prayers and in all that we do at Bethel relates to our belief that God has promised us a cancer-free zone. That is one of our number one prayers. We are focused and determined to *hit the mark*. We know that we have the ball on this one. We have seen many healed of this evil disease. We have also seen people die with this disease. But we know that as we continue to carry prayer down the field, we will hit the mark and reach the goal.

(*The Happy Intercessor*, Chapter 3)

Listen for God's voice and then pray according to His wishes and will.

Daily be committed to carry prayer down the field for the winning touchdown.

DAY 13

A Spirit Fight

And do not be conformed to this world, but be transformed by the renewing of your mind, that you may prove what is that good and acceptable and perfect will of God (Romans 12:2).

DEVOTION

We know this is a spirit fight. One of the things that we are pushing against is a worldly mindset. I think of a worldly mindset as a humanistic, self-focused, carnal mindset that is not set on the things of God. The more we pray, read the Bible, preach, and "do" by healing the sick, the more we break down that mindset.

Jesus did this very thing. He showed us how to spirit-fight. He broke down that worldly mindset by praying, preaching, and doing. One specific way that He broke down that mindset was by healing the sick. If someone you know does not believe that God heals, but witnesses a sick person being made whole after you lay your hands on them, this can break through the mindset of the unbelieving heart. We have seen that happen many times—where a person who didn't believe in healing became a believer after watching God heal someone.

(*The Happy Intercessor*, Chapter 3)

REFLECTIONS

1. What is the first thing that comes to your mind when you read
   or hear the phrase "spirit fight"? *Pray - read & claim*
   Scripture

2. Do you have a worldly mindset—a humanistic, self-focused,
   carnal mindset that is not set on the things of God.
   Too often

3. How can you break down that type of mindset?
   Pray
   Preach
   doing — (healing sick etc.)

4. Jesus broke down worldly mindsets by healing the sick and
   making believers out of unbelievers.

5. Do you believe people today can heal the sick through the power
   of the Holy Spirit? *YES!*

MEDITATIVE ACTION

At Bethel Church, my job is to oversee the prayer. As the Prayer Pastor, I get a lot of emails from all around the world. Many of the emails are asking for emergency prayer or have a high prayer alert. Many are good, but many are so full of fear that I must reject the spirit that is attached to them. I refuse to pray out of fear. What I *will* do is stop and ask God how to pray about the crisis and for His direction. I stay focused on God and not on the crisis.

When you move your prayers into fear, you can't possibly get a clear handle on how to pray according to how Heaven is praying. We must be like the sons of Issachar; we must understand and know what to do. Staying focused and keeping to the plan is most important.

(*The Happy Intercessor*, Chapter 3)

Rather than immediately reacting to an urgent prayer request, take time to consider any negative spirit that may accompany the request.

Devise a personally intimate plan to help keep you focused on God and not on every crisis that comes at you.

DAY 14

Bloodshed

Because you have plundered many nations, all the remnant of the people shall plunder you, because of men's blood and the violence of the land and the city.... "Woe to him who builds a town with bloodshed, who establishes a city by iniquity!" (Habakkuk 2:8,12)

DEVOTION

Several years ago, there was a brutal murder in our city. Two young men murdered two other men just because they were homosexuals. I woke up that next morning and read the paper to hear that this had taken place in our county. I was saddened by the news. I went up to our prayer house and wept before God. I asked for forgiveness for the murders that we had committed in our city. I cried for mercy, that God would heal our land from the bloodshed.

You see, as an intercessor, it is my job to take ownership over what takes place in this area. You might say, "Wait a minute, you obviously didn't commit the crime, so why are you taking the blame?" Because I have taken "ownership" over my land, I take it personally when something takes place in this area that is sinful and wrong. If something has gone wrong, I see it as my responsibility to make it right through confession and repentance.

(*The Happy Intercessor*, Chapter 4)

REFLECTIONS

1. Have you ever been so saddened by the news that you have prayed and wept before God?

2. Have you cried for mercy, that God would heal your land from the bloodshed?

3. Have you taken ownership over the sin that has overtaken your community, state, nation?

4. Is it your responsibility to make things right through confession and repentance?

5. How does this responsibility fit in with being a "happy" intercessor?

MEDITATIVE ACTION

One day while praying, I felt as if the Lord told me to pray for the government. The feeling was that it was a long-term prayer target, something I would pray for the rest of my life—so much so that my first email address had "prayfor5" in it. One of the meanings for the number *five* is the fivefold government. What kind of government did God want me to pray for? The three key areas are: (1) physical government of our nation, (2) the spiritual government of our area, and (3) the fivefold governmental offices of the Church—apostle, prophet, evangelists, pastor, and teacher.

It has been more than 12 years, and the prayer subject has not changed. These are still three key areas in my life. These areas of prayer have led to some amazing adventures. God has brought many people with kindred spirits to help with this adventure. The strategies and prophetic acts that have transpired have been so fun and active and full of Holy Spirit energy.

(*The Happy Intercessor*, Chapter 4)

Listen quietly. Has the Lord told you to pray for something or someone regional, national, or worldwide?

Write three strategies that you can put into practice that comply with what God has told you.

DAY 15

For Others

For He made Him who knew no sin to be sin for us, that we might become the righteousness of God in Him (2 Corinthians 5:21).

For what the law could not do in that it was weak through the flesh, God did by sending His own Son in the likeness of sinful flesh, on account of sin: He condemned sin in the flesh...(Romans 8:3).

DEVOTION

There are many examples in the Bible of intercessors—the greatest being Jesus. When Jesus said, *"It is finished"* (John 19:30), that was the end of His intercession here on earth. Remember, an intercessor pleads with somebody in authority on behalf of somebody else, especially someone who is to be punished. Jesus is our intercession. He stands between God and human sin. Not only does He stand on our behalf, but He also became sin to redeem us.

In Shasta County, there is a two-and-a-half-month harvest season for marijuana. Because a lot of Shasta County is remote and in the foothills of the north end of the state of California, there is quite a lot of marijuana grown, not just in our county, but also in the counties all around us. It is a big business. The money that is brought in from the growth of marijuana is, in turn, used to make other drugs. When I was a teacher's aide many years ago, all of the teachers had to take a drug abuse awareness and prevention education class. They told us that marijuana was the gateway drug, that when you start using marijuana, it was only a matter of time before you experimented with other drugs. It is also the drug that gives you the money to buy more dangerous drugs.

REFLECTIONS

1. An intercessor pleads with somebody in authority on behalf of somebody else, especially someone who is to be punished. Do you know someone in need of an intercessor?

2. When Jesus died on the cross for you—that was the end of His intercession here on earth. Do you realize that He is still interceding for you?

3. How clear is it to you that not only does He stand on your behalf, but He also became sin to redeem you?

4. Is there a drug problem in your community, your school, your home?

5. Has your family been affected by the use and abuse of illegal drugs by someone you know or love?

MEDITATIVE ACTION

A woman in our church told me that one of her sons wanted to talk to me about the drug business in our area. This young man was not saved and was a drug runner himself. I agreed to meet with him and talk. He began to tell me many interesting things about our area and what was going on. It was very informative and gave me some insight that stirred me up for prayer. I asked God to show me how to pray with a strategy.

(*The Happy Intercessor*, Chapter 4)

Take the time to talk with someone who knows about the drug problems in your neighborhood—a policeman, a drug counselor, perhaps.

Pray as God leads you to intercede for the drug addicts, those trying to help them, and the families whose lives have been disrupted and/or destroyed.

DAY 16

Taking Ownership

But if you are led by the Spirit, you are not under the law. Now the works of the flesh are evident, which are: adultery, fornication, uncleanness, lewdness, idolatry, sorcery, hatred, contentions, jealousies, outbursts of wrath, selfish ambitions, dissensions, heresies (Galatians 5:18-20).

DEVOTION

One of the ministries here in our city has done a great job in bringing city leaders and spiritual city leaders together. We meet from time to time to have lunch and talk. At one of these meetings, our sheriff was asked to share about what is happening in our city. Not everything he talked about was good news that day. But it was good to hear so that we would pray more effectively as spiritual leaders. One good thing he talked about was the way that the police department has been working to fight against the drug problem in our city. He told us that they had just completed an operation to harvest marijuana plants. In two weeks, they had harvested 284,000 plants, and by the season's end they were projecting 365,000 plants. Five thousand plants bring in $1.6 billion.

There are three verses in the Bible that talk about sorcery: Second Chronicles 33:6, Galatians 5:20, and Revelation 18:23. When we prayed that day up on the border, we were right on track. Once again we were taking ownership. We were asking for a cleansing to happen over the land.

(*The Happy Intercessor*, Chapter 4)

REFLECTIONS

1. Second Chronicles 33:6 says, *"Also he caused his sons to pass through the fire in the Valley of the Son of Hinnom; he practiced soothsaying, used witchcraft and sorcery, and consulted mediums and spiritists. He did much evil in the sight of the LORD, to provoke Him to anger."* Do you knowingly or unknowingly practice sorcery? Do you consult the daily horoscopes, consult psychics?

2. Consider Revelation 18:23: *"The light of a lamp shall not shine in you anymore, and the voice of bridegroom and bride shall not be heard in you anymore. For your merchants were the great men of the earth, for by your sorcery all the nations were deceived."* Write what you believe sorcery means in this Scripture verse.

3. How does the love of money control the drug problem that permeates the nation?

4. Can prayer and taking ownership make a difference in your community?

5. Is this situation so immense that you feel too overwhelmed to start a prayer campaign against it?

MEDITATIVE ACTION

This makes so much sense and gives us understanding into the life of drug addiction. It is like a spell. As we pray over those we love who are addicted and caught in that curse of the devil, let's remember to address the sorcery that has come to destroy them. Let us be the go-between for those we know who are living in addictions.

(*The Happy Intercessor*, Chapter 4).

Write a list of people you know are addicted to drugs—pray earnestly and deliberately for their freedom.

Choose one person from that list to focus on directly with occasional phone calls, notes, meals, etc., in addition to prayer.

DAY 17

Jesus, Our Joy

Looking unto Jesus, the author and finisher of our faith, who for the joy that was set before Him endured the cross, despising the shame, and has sat down at the right hand of the throne of God (Hebrews 12:2).

DEVOTION

We were sitting at the table eating our Easter breakfast, but Brian was having a hard time eating his eggs because he had spotted the cinnamon rolls over on the stove. Reasoning with him just wasn't working, so Bill, being a man full of wisdom, picked Brian up with his plate of eggs, walked over to the stove, and said, "Brian if you eat your eggs, you can have a cinnamon roll." So Brian sat there in Bill's arms eating his eggs, all the time staring at the cinnamon rolls. When he finished, he got his roll. He had endured the cross (eggs) for the joy (roll) set before him. This may be a silly story, but it does illustrate a good point.

Intercessors should be the happiest people on the planet because they know the plans of God. God is in a good mood, and He wants to give good gifts to His children. As intercessors, our job is to look ahead to the good gifts that God wants to give to us and to agree with those plans. As intercessors, we have to be OK with the fact that God is OK with *motivating* us with gifts. We can see this in the Scriptures.

(*The Happy Intercessor*, Chapter 5)

REFLECTIONS

1. Intercessors should be the happiest people on the planet because they know the plans of God. Are you?

2. God is in a good mood, and He wants to give good gifts to His children. Are you willing to receive His good gifts?

3. As an intercessor, you are to look ahead to the good gifts that God wants to give and to agree with His plans. Are you looking ahead? Why or why not?

4. How does God motivate you with gifts? When was the last time you felt motivated by God?

5. Do you experience joy in your heart when you think of Jesus? Are you happy most days? Do people see you and think, *Wow, I wish I could be as genuinely cheerful as that person!*

MEDITATIVE ACTION

Jesus endured so much while He was here on earth, and He endured it for the *promise of joy* that was set before Him. Jesus is into *joy!* The King of kings and Lord of lords became a man, which was His choosing. And He endured it all for joy. That, in itself, was enough to give Him all of the endurance He needed—enduring the suffering of just being in a man's body after living in the heavenly realm full of light, power, and joy! In my opinion, the joy is what kept Him enduring the earthly living and the dying.

(The Happy Intercessor, Chapter 5)

Determine that Jesus will be your example and that you will endure whatever comes your way as joy.

Know that you can endure the suffering and the challenges because Jesus personally provided you the power to do so.

DAY 18

Wear a Smile

If I say, "I will forget my complaint, I will put off my sad face and wear a smile" (Job 9:27).

DEVOTION

We have an elementary school at our church in Redding. Every year they have a program in the form of dance and drama. It's about creation, the life of Jesus, and the war between the demonic realm and angelic realm. One of the scenes shows the angels standing in Heaven watching as Jesus is being accused, beaten, and eventually crucified on the cross. The angels are so disturbed because they have been given instructions not to come to His defense. At no other time had they been prevented from helping Jesus. The Scriptures say He endured this because of the joy (see Heb. 12:2).

We believe, as a people of God's power, that we are to bring Heaven to earth. Joy is a very big part of Heaven. Heaven is filled with joy. It is our responsibility to bring that here on earth.

(*The Happy Intercessor*, Chapter 5)

REFLECTIONS

1. If I say, *"I will forget my complaint, I will put off my sad face and wear a smile"* (Job 9:27). What complaints are you willing to forget about?

2. If I say, *"I will forget my complaint, I will put off my sad face and wear a smile"* (Job 9:27). Are you willing to put off your sad face and wear a smile instead?

3. Why weren't the angels permitted to help Jesus?

4. *"looking unto Jesus, the author and finisher of our faith, who for the joy that was set before Him endured the cross, despising the shame, and has sat down at the right hand of the throne of God"* (Heb. 12:2). Write what you imagine "the joy that was set before Him" looked and felt like.

5. Write what you imagine the joy of Heaven looks and feels like.

MEDITATIVE ACTION

There is no depression in Heaven, so we have no legal right to depression. If you are depressed, you need to recheck your life. Figure out why, and for Heaven and earth's sake, take care of it. The world needs to see happy, joyful, alive people of God who love and serve out of joy.

What comes with Jesus' completeness on the cross is that we can now fight *from* victory not *for* victory. We as intercessors are praying and begging God for things that are already ours because of what Jesus did on the cross.

(*The Happy Intercessor*, Chapter 5)

Get serious about your outlook on life. Acknowledge and own the joy that Jesus brought with Him.

Stop fighting *for* victory and start fighting *from* victory!

DAY 19

But What About…

Take My yoke upon you and learn from Me, for I am gentle and lowly in heart, and you will find rest for your souls. For My yoke is easy and My burden is light (Matthew 11:29-30).

DEVOTION

You might be thinking, *But what about all the horrible stuff that is going on in the world? Shouldn't that affect us?* Yes, it should.

I met with a woman in our church who wanted to tell me about some things going on in our city with the occult. After we met, I headed right over to our prayer house. I was feeling a little weighty and needed to get God's perception on all that I had heard.

As I walked in the prayer garden, I had a vision. In the vision, I was in a familiar place with Jesus. We were walking and holding hands. It felt like we were sharing intimate secrets. I was talking to Him about the information I had just received. I looked over at His other hand, which was closed. I could tell that He was holding something in secret in that hand. I asked Him what He had in His hand. He opened His hand, and I saw that He was holding the whole world. It looked so small. When I saw that, all of the heaviness left, and I realized that He has everything under His control and in His hand.

Now, that doesn't mean that I don't continue to pray over these matters for my city. But it does mean that I can't carry the heaviness. See, Jesus already did that. He carried it all to the cross.

(*The Happy Intercessor*, Chapter 5)

REFLECTIONS

1. Do you often wonder about all the horrible things happening in the world? Do you allow your thoughts to be consumed with sadness?

2. Do you take time to get God's perception on all that you hear, read, and see?

3. Have you ever held the hand of Jesus and talked over what is on your mind?

4. Do you believe that Jesus has you by one hand and the world in His other hand?

5. Only the Trinity can handle all the heaviness caused by sin in this world. Share your burdens with Jesus—He is more than joyful to lighten your load.

MEDITATIVE ACTION

It's very important that, as intercessors, we have a revelation of what Jesus did while He was here on the earth. Jesus came to set the captive free. He healed the sick, raised the dead, and cast out demons (see Luke 4:18). If we continually carry around an attitude of sorrows, lugging around what Jesus already carried to the cross (all of the sins and feelings that go with that sorrow), then we are denying what Jesus did for all humankind.

Did you notice the word, "carry"? I'm speaking to those who "carry" the weight and heaviness of another person around even though Jesus already carried it to the cross for us. Jesus said, "It is finished!" My husband has a sermon message with this statement, "What part of finished don't you understand?" If we can catch this thought and put it into our hearts, our prayer lives will change. We will become confident in what Jesus did, and we will become releasers of His Kingdom here on earth.

(*The Happy Intercessor*, Chapter 5)

Believe that Jesus came to set the captive free, heal the sick, raise the dead, and cast out demons. He did this then—and He continues to love us this way today.

Ask yourself: What part of *finished* don't you understand?

DAY 20

The Joy of the Lord

His lord said to him, "Well done, good and faithful servant; you were faithful over a few things, I will make you ruler over many things. Enter into the joy of your lord" (Matthew 25:21).

DEVOTION

In the movie, *The Passion*, there is a scene where Jesus is at His home building a table. His mother comes out, and they are laughing together. That's one of my favorite parts of the movie. I know it's something the writer added to the movie, but I can imagine that that is how Jesus lived. I believe Jesus laughed a lot and enjoyed life. He was able to bring the joy of Heaven to earth.

If we feed ourselves on life and joy and what God is doing here on earth, we will live like Jesus lived on earth. But, if we feed ourselves on bad news all of the time, if that is our focus in life, then we will live out of fear and despair.

I like to imagine. God has given us a wonderful tool: our imaginations. When I read the stories in the Bible, I use my imagination to look at the whole story. What do you see when you read about Jesus healing the sick? When the eyes of the blind were opened and the person who had been deaf all his life could hear for the first time, there was joy and excitement. This is where we need to live. We are releasers of Heaven and all that Heaven holds.

(*The Happy Intercessor*, Chapter 5)

REFLECTIONS

1. Can you imagine that Jesus laughed a lot and enjoyed life?

2. Do you feed on bad news and then live out of fear and despair?

3. Use your imagination to look at Bible stories. What do you see when you read about Jesus healing the little girl, the blind man, the woman with the issue of blood?

4. You are a releaser of Heaven and all that Heaven holds. What does that mean to you?

5. Write several examples of the joy of the Lord experienced in your life.

   1. Joy experienced during worship
   2. " when hear of salvations
   3. " "read scriptures
   4. " in beautiful nature
   5. " w/ animals
   6. " Majestic Music
   7. " friendships

MEDITATIVE ACTION

Talk about a life of joy. When we travel to different parts of the world, we have the joy of praying for hundreds of people. One of the things that I like the most is seeing people hear that God is in a good mood and that He wants to bless them. When they understand that, they have authority to do the stuff that Jesus did, and they begin to use their authority for the first time. Watching them pray for the sick and see someone healed under their hand for the first time is incredible! There in that moment is much joy.

(*The Happy Intercessor*, Chapter 5)

Choose to be in a good mood today—all day. Then determine to be in a good mood tomorrow—and every day after that.

Determine that you have been given the authority to be God's representative on earth. Take that responsibility seriously.

DAY 21

The Three Realms

*I know a man in Christ who fourteen years ago—
whether in the body I do not know, or whether out of
the body, I do not know, God knows—such a one was
caught up to the* **third heaven** *(2 Corinthians 12:2).*

Now I saw a new heaven and a new earth, for the **first
heaven** *and the first earth had passed away. Also there
was no more sea (Revelation 21:1).*

Indeed heaven and the **highest heavens** *belong to
the Lord your God, also the earth with all that is in it
(Deuteronomy 10:14).*

And I saw another angel flying in **midheaven,** *having
an eternal gospel to preach to those who live on the
earth and to every nation and tribe and tongue and
people (Revelation 14:6 NASB)*

DEVOTION

There are three "realms" mentioned in the Bible. The word *realm* means a region, sphere, or area. The Bible specifically talks about the first realm, the second realm, and the third realm. The first realm is the realm that you can see with your eyes. It's the physical realm (see Rev. 21:1). So here you can see that the first heaven is the earthly realm, or what you can see right now. Our bodies, our homes, and our cities exist in the earthly realm. (see Deut. 10:14).

The second heaven, or "mid-heaven" of Revelation 14:6 is the demonic and angelic realm where they war with each other. In Daniel, the second realm is also shown to be the demonic and angelic realm (see Dan. 10:13). The third realm, or highest heaven, is where we find the paradise of God (see 2 Cor. 12:2-4).

(*The Happy Intercessor*, Chapter 6)

REFLECTIONS

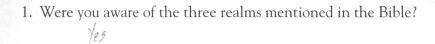

1. Were you aware of the three realms mentioned in the Bible?

   Yes

2. Where do you mostly live? In the first, second, or third realm?

   1st

3. In which realm do you feel the most "at home"?

   3rd ?

4. Is there anything you can do to make the third realm more comfortable? More natural?

   spend more time there?

5. In which realm did Jesus live? Mary? Paul? Judas? Pilate? Job? David?

MEDITATIVE ACTION

The problem is that, when intercessors choose to pray from those realms, they end up praying from a defensive place. This is what it looks like. You are watching television or reading the newspaper and some bad news comes across. You have just been made aware of the first realm (the physical realm). You become defensive in your prayers and pray on a human level. Or, you see into the demonic realm. Something bad is afoot. Sometimes it feels like pressure, like you have to pray now. It feels like you are chasing after the devil, and if you don't pray now, the whole world will be destroyed. I know that's a little extreme, but you get the idea.

(*The Happy Intercessor*, Chapter 6)

Decide to pray only from the third realm. Place yourself in the third realm so you can be the most effective intercessor possible.

DAY 22

The Spirit Realm

*But to the Son He says: "Your throne, O God, is for-
ever and ever; a scepter of righteousness is the scepter of Your kingdom. You have loved righteousness
and hated lawlessness; therefore God, Your God, has
anointed You with the oil of gladness more than Your
companions"* (Hebrews 1:8-9).

DEVOTION

When I began this journey into intercession, I didn't say, "OK, I'm going to be an intercessor now." Instead, I simply fell into the third realm of Heaven, and I fell madly in love with the Holy Spirit. I touched a realm that I had never experienced before. I am now so very addicted to His presence; His realm is where I always want to dwell.

One of the things that we have felt, in all of our travels, is the importance of carrying His joy wherever we go. That is our assignment from Heaven. Remember there is great joy in Heaven, and that is our model for life and ministry here on earth.

Because Jesus loved righteousness and hated lawlessness, God gave Him the oil of gladness (see Heb. 1:9). He had more joy than all of His brethren. He even endured the cross because of the joy set before Him. This tells us that joy is one of Heaven's greatest treasures.

(*The Happy Intercessor*, Chapter 6)

REFLECTIONS

1. Have you fallen into the third realm of Heaven and madly in love with the Holy Spirit?

2. Is it really possible to dwell in this realm of Heaven?

3. The great joy in Heaven is your model for life and ministry here on earth. Do you agree?

4. Hebrews 1:9 says, "You [Jesus] have loved righteousness and hated lawlessness; therefore God, Your God, has anointed You with the oil of gladness more than Your companions." What does this verse mean to you?

5. If joy is one of Heaven's greatest treasures, what are some other treasures?

MEDITATIVE ACTION

When we hang around in the presence of Jesus, we will come into contact with that joy. Have you noticed that a couple who has been married a long time begins to look like each other? And, they can even act like each other. The more we spend time with Jesus, the more we will become like Him. You want more joy? Do what that psalmist did in Psalm 73. He went before God. He poured out his heart to God; he found God's presence. We need to go before God and stay there until we feel Him and are changed.

(The Happy Intercessor, Chapter 6)

What steps can you take today to make you become more like Jesus?

Read Psalm 73 several times, then pour out your heart until you experience God's presence.

DAY 23

The Third Realm

*I know a man in Christ who fourteen years ago—
whether in the body I do not know, or whether out of
the body, I do not know, God knows—such a one was
caught up to the **third heaven** (2 Corinthians 12:2).*

DEVOTION

The third realm is where the glory of God is. It's the beauty realm. Apostle Paul calls the third heaven "paradise." It's where we can see the great plans of Heaven.

He continues in verse 4, "*...how he was caught up into Paradise and heard inexpressible words....*"

The third realm is where every believer should live. You see, all believers should live from a place of victory, knowing and partnering with the strategies of God. Ephesians 2:6 says that God has "*raised us up together, and made us sit together in the heavenly places in Christ Jesus.*" You have heard the saying, "so heavenly minded no earthy good"? That's a very impossible saying. I believe that, if you are heavenly minded, you will be of great good to this earth.

(*The Happy Intercessor*, Chapter 6)

REFLECTIONS

1. Are you aware of the three realms and that the third realm is where the glory of God is?

2. Do you live in the third realm—a place of victory, knowing, and partnering with the strategies of God?

3. Do you realize that God has raised you up to sit together in the heavenly places in Christ Jesus?

4. Has someone ever referred to you saying that you are so heavenly minded that you are no earthy good?

5. As Paul, have you ever been "caught up to the third heaven"?

MEDITATIVE ACTION

I've discovered that many intercessors do not live out of a place of joy because they get stuck in the first or second realms. When intercessors get stuck in the first realm, they are preoccupied with logic and reason. Then their prayers become focused on what *seems logical*, which is not where God is coming from most of the time! And then there are those intercessors who get stuck in the second realm. This realm is the dark and demonic realm, which produces hopelessness, doom, and fear.

(*The Happy Intercessor*, Chapter 6)

Get unstuck from the first realm by balancing logic and reason.

Get unstuck from the second realm by denouncing the devil and avoiding his traps and temptations.

DAY 24

Airways

*In which you once walked according to the course of this world, according to the **prince of the power of the air,** the spirit who now works in the sons of disobedience (Ephesians 2:2).*

DEVOTION

Those who own the airways control the atmosphere. The *airways* are the spiritual climate over a city. It is our responsibility to take ownership of the airways and reclaim the atmosphere. When we do that, a shift takes place in the spiritual climate in the region. When that shift takes place, we begin to see signs of revival, and entire cities become transformed by the things of God. When cities become transformed by the things of God, we see more light and less darkness in entire regions.

I'm a walker. I love to walk the land and pray and just enjoy the beauty of what God has given us. For a season, I would walk in just one area in our city. One day, during one of those walks, I felt like I was to ask the Holy Spirit what I should pray for that week. As I listened, I heard these words, "Pray for the communication lines." What I felt was that I would pray that demonic communication lines would be severed.

(*The Happy Intercessor,* Chapter 7)

REFLECTIONS

1. What does it mean to you personally to take ownership of the airways and reclaim the atmosphere?

2. Have you ever seen or been a part of a shift in the airways that changed the spiritual climate in a region?

3. Does your neighborhood, town or city need to be transformed by the things of God?

4. Has God ever asked you to "Pray for the communication lines"?

5. How many different kinds of demonic communication lines can you think of that need to be severed and completely destroyed?

MEDITATIVE ACTION

So, not really knowing how to pray, but knowing that the Holy Spirit would enlighten me for that week, I finished my walk that morning with purpose to pray into this new strategy. When I got home that day, I turned on the television to watch *Fox News*. This was during the time when the Iraq war had just started. As I turned on the television, I heard these words, "The leader who is in charge of all the communications in Iraq has been arrested." Well, to say the least, I got very excited and knew once again that the Holy Spirit was confirming His words.

What I didn't know at the time was that this strategy for prayer would become one of the most important agendas in my prayer life—breaking demonic lines and releasing the pure, godly lines of communication.

(*The Happy Intercessor,* Chapter 7)

Freedom of speech is an important right of Americans—take a stand to preserve this freedom while breaking the demonic lines that perverts this right.

Write a few strategies for releasing pure, godly lines of communication in your family, workplace, neighborhood, and/or region.

DAY 25

War in the Heavenlies

…Do not fear, Daniel, for from the first day that you set your heart to understand, and to humble yourself before your God, your words were heard; and I have come because of your words. But the prince of the kingdom of Persia withstood me twenty-one days; and behold, Michael, one of the chief princes, came to help me, for I had been left alone there with the kings of Persia (Daniel 10:12-13).

DEVOTION

In Daniel chapter 10, Daniel received a message, but he needed understanding of the message. He went to fasting for 21 days and then an angel was sent to give Daniel understanding about the message. But the ruling demonic prince held the angel back. He needed Michael, the warring angel, to come and fight this prince of Persia. The messenger angel was sent at the very beginning of Daniel's fast, but it took 21 days for the message to get through (with the help of Michael). There is a very real, invisible world around us that affects our visible world.

Now, let's take this even further so that we can understand how we can pray and allow this spirit realm to positively infect the physical world around us.

One of the beliefs that we have at Bethel is that we must infiltrate the system. We must be like good leaven. As we put ourselves into our cities as leaven, it will affect the whole city and the atmosphere as well.

(*The Happy Intercessor*, Chapter 7)

REFLECTIONS

1. Have you ever fasted for 21 days? Has an angel ever been sent to you to give you understanding about something?

2. Do you believe that fasting and angelic appearances are for to-day…or only for biblical days?

3. How firmly do you believe that there is a very real, invisible world around you that affects your visible world?

4. Do you pray and allow this spirit realm to positively infect the physical world around you?

5. On a scale from 1 to 10, what is your leavening level?

MEDITATIVE ACTION

Once, many years ago, a man who was drunk came out of the bar, got in his car, hit a young girl, and killed her. This young girl's father was a friend of one of the men in our church. The man in our church was so grieved over this loss that, driving past the bar on his way home one night, he looked over at the bar and said, "I wish that bar would burn down." That night, the bar burned down. That happened in the '70s, and from that time on, the lot stood vacant. I don't believe that praying the bar would burn down was the curse. I believe the bar being there and the atmosphere that it brought caused the land to be cursed. One day when I was praying about where to take the students, I remembered this piece of land and the story behind it. I felt like it was time that the curse be lifted off of this property. The land needed to be freed.

(*The Happy Intercessor*, Chapter 7)

Use your God-given authority to take back what the devil has been using for evil.

Take prayerful authority over the places where evil is being perpetuated and condoned.

DAY 26

Prayer Makes a Difference

Do not deprive one another except with consent for a time, that you may give yourselves to fasting and prayer; and come together again so that Satan does not tempt you because of your lack of self-control (1 Corinthians 7:5).

DEVOTION

The last day of my Advanced Ministry Training class, about 40 of us went to pray at a certain property. I gathered the students in a circle and had them declare what God was doing and, through the declaration, release the land from a curse. We believe in doing "prophetic acts" when we are praying. A prophetic act is doing something in the natural realm that brings a supernatural release. Doing an act like this causes an answer to come to the physical realm. So, we dedicated the land by pouring oil over it. We gave a shout of praise together that ended our time. I told them, "Now look for the answer."

Within a week, one of the students told me that, a few days after we prayed over our land, a gentleman went to the city's planning commission and told them that he wanted to develop that land and put homes on the property.

(*The Happy Intercessor*, Chapter 7)

REFLECTIONS

1. When is the last time you were involved in a prophetic act—doing something in the natural realm that brings a supernatural release?

2. How comfortable were you during the prophetic act? Were you embarrassed? Worried someone might see you?

3. How likely are you to do something like that by yourself rather than with a group?

4. The dramatic answer to the students' prayers was confirmation from God that He uses His children to affect change. Are you allowing Him to use you?

5. Have you given yourself to fasting and prayer so that satan doesn't tempt you because of your lack of self-control?

MEDITATIVE ACTION

Can you see what was taking place in the spirit realm? Use your imagination on this one and see what the angels were doing. They were released to do the plans of Heaven. It was like they were saying, "OK, now it's time. The curse has been broken. We now have permission to work." I can see the angels coming to the man who wanted to develop this property and whispering in his ear, "You know that idea you have about developing the corner property? Now is the time to do that."

When you work and co-partner with God, the job gets done. This was one of those times when the answer came so quickly. A clearness in the spiritual communication lines brought quick results. How exciting to see! I have to tell you, though, that I knew that there would be a release, but I didn't know it would come so fast.

(*The Happy Intercessor*, Chapter 7)

Ready yourself for swift responses to your concerted prayers.

Realize that Jesus is interceding for you and His angels are carrying messages that will make God's will be done.

DAY 27

No Words Necessary

Behold, as the eyes of servants look to the hand of their masters, as the eyes of a maid to the hand of her mistress, so our eyes look to the Lord our God, until He has mercy on us (Psalm 123:2).

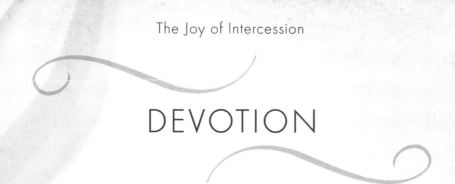

DEVOTION

I have found that there are different ways to change the atmosphere. It doesn't always have to be with words. Look at the last part of this verse, *"...so our eyes look to the Lord our God, until He has mercy on us"* (Ps. 123:2). They just kept their eyes on the Lord. No words were necessary. They just kept focused on the Lord until....

We have many beautiful mountains around our city. One time we were heading to the top of one of them to pray over our city. The view from the top of this mountain was breathtaking. There was a lookout right at the top, and we could almost see all the way around the mountain from this spot. It was a gorgeous day. There was a breeze blowing. That day, all I knew to do was to stand at the edge of the mountain and lift up my purple shawl and let it blow in the wind. So there I stood with both hands up over my head, holding my purple shawl and letting it catch the wind. Doing this was a physical prophetic act.

(*The Happy Intercessor*, Chapter 7)

REFLECTIONS

1. Have you recently looked to the Lord your God until He had mercy on you? Isn't it about time that you do?

2. When words are not necessary, what replaces that type of communication with God?

3. What is the most breathtaking scene that the good Lord has shared with you?

4. In addition to lifting up your praise and worship to God, have you raised a physical object toward Him in reverence?

5. Are you in a habit of presenting physical prophetic acts? Why or why not?

MEDITATIVE ACTION

For me, the color purple symbolizes royalty and intercession. The gold cord on the shawl was the glory around the royalty and intercession. As it blew in the wind of God, it was releasing over a region the royalty, intercession, and glory of the Kingdom. I know; it sounds a little crazy, but it sure felt good, and it was really fun. You might ask, "Did you really have to do that?" Well, maybe not, but I think that God likes what we do for Him, even if it looks a little crazy sometimes. Doing these acts may seem crazy or super-spiritual to peers; but in doing these acts, I believe that we are standing as intercessors—that we are changing the airways around us.

(*The Happy Intercessor*, Chapter 7)

Do something "crazy" for the Lord today.

Do something "super-spiritual" for the Lord today.

DAY 28

Warfare Through Worship

God is Spirit, and those who worship Him must worship in spirit and truth (John 4:24).

DEVOTION

One day I was teaching in our supernatural school about intercession. At the end of my teaching, I asked if there were any questions. One of our young men, who we would have from time to time come up on the platform to dance during our worship, made the comment that he didn't think that he was an intercessor. I looked at him and said, "Are you kidding me?" I told him that he was an intercessor and that his intercession was the dance. You see, his idea of an intercessor was one who only used words to intercede. I told him that his intercession was the worship that became the warfare.

Two elements in warfare that I feel are our greatest tools of intercession are worship and joy. I believe that these two weapons bring more confusion to the devil's camp than anything else. Both of these weapons of war come out of our intimate relationship with our Father God.

(*The Happy Intercessor,* Chapter 8)

REFLECTIONS

1. Do you *think* you are an intercessor? Do you *know* you are an intercessor?

2. Do you only use words to intercede or has the Lord given you a different gift or talent that you use?

3. Your greatest tools of intercession are worship and joy. Write what that means to you.

4. Confusing the devil by joyful worshiping the Lord keeps him away from you.

5. Worship and joy are weapons of war that come out of your intimate relationship with your Father God.

MEDITATIVE ACTION

Warfare worship is coming in on God's terms, not the devil's. We are focused on God, which ushers His power and presence into our intercessions. I was in one of our worship services one Sunday morning, and I kept getting distracted in my spirit. I felt like there were witches in the room. I found myself completely out of worship. I remember that I kept turning around to figure out what was going on. Then I heard the Holy Spirit whisper, "You are being distracted from Me; just worship Me." It was a little nudge from the Spirit, but I got it.

I realized that I needed to just be with God and worship. He would take care of the spiritual matters in the room. My weapon of warfare that morning was to worship Him. God once spoke audibly to my husband saying, "He watches over the watch of those who watch the Lord." It is clear that having our eyes fixed on Him is our most responsible position, as God watches over the things that matter to us.

(*The Happy Intercessor*, Chapter 8)

Don't be distracted—the devil's ploy is to keep you from being totally focused on your heavenly Father.

Use joyful worship to thwart all attempts by the devil to keep you from fulfilling God's will in your life.

DAY 29

Worship and God's Presence

Then Jesus said to him, "Away with you, Satan! For it is written, 'You shall worship the LORD your God, and Him only you shall serve'" (Matthew 4:10).

DEVOTION

When we worship, we can release the presence of God and His Kingdom into the room. Years ago we were doing some meetings in Alaska. For several of the meetings, during the praise and worship time, there was no worship part. The praise was good, but we weren't getting to the intimate place of worship. It felt like there was a wall between us and God. We had brought our lead dancer with us on this trip. When we want something broken in the spirit realm, we have her get up and just worship. She doesn't dance to war, but her dance of worship becomes war. After being in a couple of these services in Alaska, my husband thought that it would be a good time for her to dance. She got up and began dancing, and whatever the wall was, it disappeared, and Heaven came into the room.

There was a gentleman at that service who could see into the spiritual realm. He told us after she finished that he had been watching demons that were sitting around the room. He said that when our dancer danced, the demons began to scream, and they got out of the room as fast as they could. Even in this we do not worship because of its effect on darkness—we do so because God is worthy!

(*The Happy Intercessor*, Chapter 8)

REFLECTIONS

1. When you worship, you release the presence of God and His Kingdom. Have you felt His presence lately?

2. What is the difference between praise and an intimate place of worship?

3. Do you believe that unseen demons can be chased away by worshiping Almighty God?

4. Worship of God is for no other reason than He is worthy to be praised.

5. Worship and joy are intimately connected, *"And they worshiped Him, and returned to Jerusalem with great joy"* (Luke 24:52). How connected are you?

MEDITATIVE ACTION

Worship, in whatever form—dance, adoration that comes from our mouth, or any other kind of worship—terrifies the demonic realm. I believe they cannot stand to hear or even be close to those who are true worshipers. I've watched our son Brian take his guitar and play over a person in torment to see peace come. I know of a woman who goes to the convalescent hospital in our city and plays her flute over Alzheimer's patients to watch them become peaceful.

(*The Happy Intercessor*, Chapter 8)

Worship in a way that brings God's presence and peace to you— to another.

Worship your worthy God until the demonic realm has absolutely no control over any area of your life.

DAY 30

Watch the Children

But Jesus called them to Him and said, "Let the little children come to Me, and do not forbid them; for of such is the kingdom of God (Luke 18:16).

DEVOTION

Every year during one of our conferences, we schedule prophetic booths. People can sign up for a time to meet with a team that we have picked to prophesy over them. During the past several years we have included our children on the teams. At first people were a little skeptical until they sat down in the chair and a child would, as we say, "read their mail" and describe intimate details of their lives. Now when they come for prophetic ministry, they ask if the children are prophesying.

We have found that the kids have a purity about their prophecies—nothing extra, just raw words from Heaven. When we look back into the story of Jehoshaphat, we see that Jehoshaphat knew that the entire nation—men, women, and children—needed to be in on this prayer. It was a matter of life and death. They needed to stand together as one nation, one tribe, desperate for God to come. So God sent the prophet to tell the people what they needed to do:

> *Do not be afraid nor dismayed because of this great multitude, for the battle is not yours, but God's* (2 Chronicles 20:15).

(*The Happy Intercessor*, Chapter 8)

REFLECTIONS

1. Have you ever attended a conference that offered prophetic booths and people to prophesy over you? Are you surprised about this activity? Intrigued? Thankful?

2. Did reading about children prophesying stir your curiosity? Upset your traditional mindset? Excite your spirit?

3. Is there an issue facing your nation that you believe will take the entire population standing in unity to defeat it?

4. Do you know when to fight and when to allow God to fight your battles?

5. Has God used a child to bring you a word from Him? To show you His will? To change your perspective of a situation?

MEDITATIVE ACTION

The prophet then told them that they wouldn't have to fight in this battle but just position themselves, stand still, and see the salvation of the Lord. Jehoshaphat told the people to believe in the Lord and to believe in the prophets. He appointed those who should sing to the Lord and who should praise the beauty of holiness.

The people of God fought a war by worship. Their worship set in motion a shift in the heavenly realm, and God did the rest.

(*The Happy Intercessor*, Chapter 8)

Position yourself, stand still, sing to the Lord, and praise the beauty of holiness.

Fight the war with worship—yours is the victory.

DAY 31

Warfare Through Joy

*But now I come to You; and these things I speak in the world so that they may have **My joy** made full in themselves* (John 17:3 NASB).

DEVOTION

I believe we are to be a people who have Jesus' joy full in us. We are to be like that in every area of our life and ministry. One of the missing elements I see in many of those who are interceding is that they need their lives filled up with heavenly joy. I would love to go to Heaven for a visit and see just how joyful Heaven is. Their intercession in Heaven is not one of labor and work. There is none of that in Heaven. I think the intercession of Heaven is from a place of joy, a place of knowing.

When we head out to pray over the land, we have done our research and know that there are things that have happened there that are bad. But, we also know that God is bringing something there that will change the spiritual climate of that area. That makes us very happy. Then we are able to go out with joy and release over the land what it needs. Joy comes when you have that feeling and expectation of good coming.

(*The Happy Intercessor*, Chapter 8)

REFLECTIONS

1. Do you have Jesus' full joy in you? Why or why not?

2. Intercession is not one of labor and work—it should be joyful and rewarding.

3. Is your intercession come from a place of joy, of knowing?

4. Do you have the assurance that God is bringing something through your intercession prayers that will change the spiritual climate of that area or person?

5. Joy comes when you have the feeling and expectation of good coming. Are you joyful?

MEDITATIVE ACTION

When you use joy in your warfare, it is because you are expecting good to happen. I took my interns to a Buddhist monastery in our area. I thought it would be a good experience for them to pray in a place where another god is served. We went there to pray. I had been to this place several times before and had found it to be an easy place in which to pray. When we got there, I told them to just walk around and begin praying and feeling what God wanted to do.

While we were having this time of walking, one of my interns came told me in a singsong voice that there were a lot of demons there and that it was really easy to pray. When you experience God's presence around you, even in a demonic setting, you can find it easy to pray.

(*The Happy Intercessor*, Chapter 8)

Choose to be joyful, then go pray in a place different from your usual. Expect God's presence around you.

Write about your experience. How easy is it for you to pray when you are in a joyful mindset?

DAY 32

Rest That Is Internal

*One hand full of rest is better than two fists full of labor
and striving after wind* (Ecclesiastes 4:6 NASB).

DEVOTION

I remember one time when I felt as though I was carrying so much responsibility in prayer. One of our students came up to me one day and said that it was all right, that I didn't have to feel or carry all the responsibility of prayer. That word was so encouraging to me that day—it hit me like a breath of fresh air. I received the word and came back into a place of rest. It doesn't mean that I stopped praying for what was on my heart. But, it took me out of the striving and performance that can wrap itself around our prayer agendas (faith is more the product of surrender than it is of striving).

A mindset of performance can grab hold and push us to do things for God that He is not asking us to do. When that happens, it takes us right out of rest. We can feel like we need to do for God so that He will approve of us. We think by doing this God will accept us more and maybe love us more. I'm telling you, you don't have to do a thing for God, and He will love you no less.

(*The Happy Intercessor*, Chapter 9)

REFLECTIONS

1. Are you feeling overwhelmed with intercessory responsibilities?

2. What will it take for you to return to a place of rest?

3. Do you have a performance mindset that you need to overcome?

4. Do you feel as if you need to do for God so that He will approve of you?

5. Doing things for God makes Him love you no more or no less. Follow His lead regarding your responsibilities.

MEDITATIVE ACTION

In the Kingdom, we start off accepted. From there our identity is formed. As intercessors, we need to pray out of that new identity, that core belief that says, "I am already accepted! I am already loved! I already have favor with God!" You see, we are already accepted. Unfortunately, many of our life experiences do not teach us this. In life, you get rewarded or receive approval if you do this or that. The Kingdom of God doesn't work that way. God is not sitting up in Heaven waiting to love you if you will do something for Him. He is a lot more interested in our entering into His love and rest.

(*The Happy Intercessor*, Chapter 9)

Pray out of your new identity, the core belief that says, "I am already accepted! I am already loved! I already have favor with God!"

Realize that God is not sitting up in Heaven waiting to love you if you do this or that for Him. Enter into His love and rest.

DAY 33

True Sabbath Rest

When you were dead in your transgressions and the uncircumcision of your flesh, He [Jesus] made you alive together with Him, having forgiven us all our transgressions, having canceled out the certificate of debt consisting of decrees against us, which was hostile to us; and He has taken it out of the way, having nailed it to the cross. When He had disarmed the rulers and authorities, He made a public display of them, having triumphed over them through Him. Therefore, no one is to act as your judge in regard to food or drink or in respect to a festival or a new moon or a Sabbath day—things which are a mere shadow of what is to come; but the substance belongs to Christ (Colossians 2:13-17).

DEVOTION

The passage from Colossians 2 tells us what Jesus did when He came and gave up His life for us. He canceled the bond—all those rules and regulations that were a legal binding. It was all nailed to the cross. Principalities and powers were disarmed. Our Christ triumphed over all. So the true Sabbath becomes the rest of God. As God rested, and then as Jesus finished His work and rested, we too can enter into a true rest.

> There remains therefore a **rest** for the people of God. For he who has entered His **rest** has himself also ceased from his works as God did from His (Hebrews 4:9-10).

I believe that the true Shabbat rest means to cease from your labors, your own efforts, your own activities. I am not implying that you stop your ministry or working for the Kingdom. What I am telling you is that you must have the heart of rest. That means ceasing from your own efforts, your own striving, and depending on the works of another: God. Whenever I begin to get that overwhelming feeling and I feel the striving coming on, I stop myself and enter right back into the rest of the Lord. When we walk in this rest, we live our lives more fully, and we are more effective in our ministries and giftings.

(*The Happy Intercessor*, Chapter 9)

REFLECTIONS

1. As God rested, and then as Jesus finished His work and rested, you too can enter into a true rest. Have you done so lately?

2. What does having "the heart of rest" mean to you?

3. Is your heart at rest?

4. Have you ceased your own efforts, your own striving, and do you depend on the works of God?

5. Are you walking in this rest, living your life more fully, and being more effective in your ministries and giftings?

MEDITATIVE ACTION

As intercessors, if we want to stay in a place of rest, we have to learn how to pray and do our part and to then give our burdens back to the Lord.

I believe it is possible to carry rest with us because God is not asking us to carry the world on our shoulders. He is asking us to enter into a rest that is internal. My husband is, I think, one of the busiest people on the planet. It is a challenge for him to get the rest he needs. But, the one thing that I have noticed through our years together is that he carries an internal rest of the Lord. It is very strong in him. He knows where his Source is, and he draws from it often. If he didn't have that inner strength, there is no way that he could carry on with his life. We have no plan "B." God is our plan "A," and He is our Source.

(The Happy Intercessor, Chapter 9)

Stay in the place of rest and learn how to give your burdens to the Lord.

Carry God's internal rest with you wherever you go.

DAY 34

Resting in the Storm

Now when He got into a boat, His disciples followed Him. And suddenly a great tempest arose on the sea, so that the boat was covered with the waves. But He was asleep. Then His disciples came to Him and awoke Him, saying, "Lord, save us! We are perishing!" But He said to them, "Why are you fearful, O you of little faith?" Then He arose and rebuked the winds and the sea, and there was a great calm. So the men marveled, saying, "Who can this be, that even the winds and the sea obey Him" (Matthew 8:23-27).

DEVOTION

As we read this story in Matthew 8, we have to wonder how Jesus slept in a storm when it looked like all were going to perish. Jesus even asked them after they cried out to Him, *"Why are you fearful, O you of little faith"* (Matt. 8:26). Jesus lived in an internal security. It was so strong in Him that nothing could shake Him from that reality. Jesus could sleep in a storm. He practiced and modeled for us in this story, giving us an example of what it looks like to have rest of the heart. But even though we can carry the rest of God with us, we still have to learn how to *enter* His rest.

I remember one of the first times that I began to practice moving into the rest of God. It was a few years ago, and I had driven into town to do some shopping. On that hour-long drive, the vehicle that I was driving decided to give up and quit. My first response was to panic and get really mad. "How could this happen? Everything is now messed up for the day." You know how we carry on sometimes. I found a pay phone (no cell phones then) to call my husband. As I began to dial the number, I thought to myself, "Why am I acting this way? Why am I so upset?" Then I realized something that was so simple but that changed my life. I thought, *If I settle down and come to rest inside, I will be able to see what God can do in this situation.* Of course, once I made that decision, everything lined up and worked together. I chose the "rest of the Lord" that day for my life. I think about that day often. In what seemed like a trivial thing, God let me see that I could draw from His rest anytime I needed. It was my choice.

(*The Happy Intercessor,* Chapter 9)

REFLECTIONS

1. Jesus lived in an internal security. It was so strong in Him that nothing could shake Him from that reality. How easy is it for you to live in a state of internal security?

2. Have you learned how to enter His rest?

3. Do you allow trivial things to upset you, your day, your plans?

4. How flexible are you? Can you adjust quickly to a change in plans?

5. Learning how to adapt to changing situations usually means looking to God for His strength and stability.

MEDITATIVE ACTION

Have you ever play the "what if" game? For example, what if the disciples would have made a choice and stepped right into that rest that Jesus had? What would have happened in this story? What if you step right into the "rest of the Lord" right now? What would happen? The story of your life would be quite different, wouldn't it be?

God is calling us to choose His rest and to cultivate it in all that we do.

(*The Happy Intercessor*, Chapter 9)

Play the "what if" game the next time you face a circumstance that upsets you.

Step into the "rest of the Lord" right now.

DAY 35

Addressing the Issues

Now I beg you, brethren, through the Lord Jesus Christ, and through the love of the Spirit, that you strive together with me in prayers to God for me, that I may be delivered from those in Judea who do not believe, and that my service for Jerusalem may be acceptable to the saints (Romans 15:30-31).

DEVOTION

The ministry of intercessory prayer within the church is a helping ministry. We as intercessors are to pray for the pastors and leaders as well as the ministries of the church. We are there to bless the leadership, to pray over their ministries that they would expand and be blessed and grow, and to pray for protection over them and their families. As intercessors, we are there to make things easier for the leaders. That's what we felt like we were doing. We felt like we were helping.

(*The Happy Intercessor*, Chapter 10)

REFLECTIONS

1. Because the ministry of intercessory prayer within the church is a helping ministry, are you fulfilling your role to the best of your God-given ability?

2. Are you praying for the pastors and leaders as well as the ministries of your church?

3. Do you consistently pray for the leadership to be blessed, grow, and for protection over them and their families?

4. Are you making things easier for them?

5. How focused on helping are your prayers?

MEDITATIVE ACTION

During this time, we felt like we were to have intercessors praying during the services. We set up intercessors to cover the worship team and to cover the speaker during the services. We were praying for blessing, for the anointing, and for God to come. So we started assigning people to pray behind the stage on Sundays. God was just pouring out, and we were agreeing with Him, and we didn't want to miss out on anything that He was doing. Those intercessors became a covering for the worship team as well as the speaker for that Sunday.

(*The Happy Intercessor*, Chapter 10)

Seek out those who may feel a special calling to pray for specific ministries in your church.

Become one who prays specifically for a leader, worship team member, children's teacher, etc.

DAY 36

Confronting Bad Dreams

It is the glory of God to conceal a matter, but the glory of kings is to search out a matter (Proverbs 25:2).

DEVOTION

I remember that a lot of people started picking up "negative things" during that season of my life. I think of negative things as dreams, visions, and thoughts that do not reveal the plans that God has to bless the earth.

You see, people were picking up dreams, visions, and thoughts from the second realm. People were coming to me with so much negativity that I felt like we were not seeing correctly. When I went to the Holy Spirit for counsel and understanding, I felt like He told me that He was allowing this information to come out because He wanted us to learn how to pray from Heaven's perspective.

So when people would come to me with the negative, second realm feelings and insights, I would tell them that God was allowing them to see this for a reason. It was now their responsibility to see this from Heaven's perspective. I told them that they needed to ask God what He was up to. When you see something negative, you always need to go to God and say, "OK, God, what are you doing? What are you saying through this? How do you want me to pray?"

(*The Happy Intercessor*, Chapter 10)

REFLECTIONS

1. Negative things are dreams, visions, and thoughts that do not reveal the plans that God has to bless the earth. Can you list 2-3 negative things that you are aware of in your community, your church?

2. Have you ever been presented with so much negativity that you started to doubt God? Yourself?

3. Rather than dwelling on the negative, have you learned how to pray from Heaven's perspective?

4. It is up to you to ask God what He is up to. Have you?

5. How recently have you said, "OK, God, what are You doing? What are You saying through this? How do You want me to pray?"

MEDITATIVE ACTION

Let me give you an example of searching out the treasure. One Sunday morning, I found myself on the floor with God. He brought a picture of a man who owned one of the tattoo parlors in town. The eyes tell you all you need to know. I saw the hate and anger. Instead of cursing the man and cursing his business, I began to see God's heart for him. Oh my, I was so undone.

I prayed his destiny over him and prayed for God to pour His love out on him and to take the hate and anger. I have never heard if that young man changed his ways or if the hate and anger left. But, because of the intense time of prayer, I know that God was up to something that morning. I was the one standing in the gap for that man, pleading his case before God. Allow God to grab your heart. Let Him take you to a place of intercession. Be still and know that He is God. When I was praying for that young man, I was seeing him the way God saw him. It's what we call "finding the gold in someone."

(*The Happy Intercessor*, Chapter 10)

When God brings a person to your mind, pray for that person—stand in the gap for him or her.

Plead the case for a person in your neighborhood you know is not a believer, seeing him or her as God sees the person.

DAY 37

Intercessory Fun

Likewise the Spirit also helps in our weaknesses. For we do not know what we should pray for as we ought, but the Spirit Himself makes intercession for us with groanings which cannot be uttered (Romans 8:26).

DEVOTION

We have a large group of organized intercessors within the church. Our intercessors are taught to wait for the Holy Spirit and to ask for His leading.

One of the things that is so fun about our intercessors' meetings is that, because our intercessors wait on the direction of the Holy Spirit before they begin to pray, every meeting is different. The Holy Spirit is so progressive and creative! Our intercessors spend time soaking in the presence of the Holy Spirit before they begin to pray. They wait on Him as they prepare their bodies, souls, and spirits to work together as one. Our intercessors find out what He is doing before they begin to pray.

I believe that one of the things that makes our groups of intercessors so successful is that they have trust and honor from the leadership within the church. Through relationship, we know as leaders that we can turn this ministry over to a group of very devoted people, and we know that they will carry our vision.

(*The Happy Intercessor*, Chapter 10)

REFLECTIONS

1. Have you been taught to wait for the Holy Spirit and to ask for His leading?

2. Have you witnessed the Holy Spirit being progressive and creative? In what ways?

3. What does it mean to you to spend time soaking in the presence of the Holy Spirit before you begin to pray?

4. As an intercessor, do you feel trust and honor from the leadership within your church?

5. Can you be trusted to carry your leadership's vision?

MEDITATIVE ACTION

Pastors, I encourage you to honor and develop trust with those in your church who are intercessors. They may be a little wild and seem to do some crazy, symbolic, prophetic stuff, but if you will give them covering and let them fly, they will be dedicated to you to the death. Intercessors, if you will come under your leadership and submit your ministry of prayer and service, you will find fulfillment that you have been longing for. A successful relationship between pastors and intercessors is worth working for.

(*The Happy Intercessor*, Chapter 10)

Have fun while waiting on the Lord. Be open to what the Lord desires of you.

Pastors and intercessors, work together to bring God's will into every encounter.

DAY 38

Mystics and Contemplatives

Your way, O God, is in the sanctuary
(Psalm 77:13).

DEVOTION

This day is dedicated to the mystics, the contemplatives, those now and those who have gone on before us, those who have lived in deep communion with the Three-ness, the Trinity. The mystics call their communion, "ecstasies." My hope and prayer is that you will experience the realms of ecstasy, the realms where you are called to the deep places of God, and that His water will flow over you.

> *True contemplatives do not seek unusual experiences, much less personal power. Their consuming goal is intimacy with God.*
> —Dame Julian of Norwich

I've found myself being drawn to learning as much as I can about the mystics. To me, "mystics" are the people who have laid down their entire lives to seek after one thing, the very heart of God. One thing that makes "mystics" different from other people is that they have only one desire, to know God in His fullness.

(*The Happy Intercessor*, Chapter 11)

REFLECTIONS

1. Have you ever experienced realms of ecstasy, the realms where you are called to the deep places of God?

2. Do you consider yourself a mystic? Why or why not?

3. Do you seek with all of your being the very heart of God?

4. Do you know someone who is a mystic? What makes that person different from others who love God?

5. Is it even possible for human beings to know God in His fullness?

MEDITATIVE ACTION

Mystics are not satisfied with what is in front of them. They want to see more. Mystics see beyond this reality and into the spirit realm.

To them, God is more real than life. God is their life. Mystics see how the spirit realm connects with the worldly realms. In other words, they see how and where Heaven is invading earth. They take all of those connections, and they put them together and make sense of it all. Mystics are able to see into the spiritual realm and use it to help define what is going on in the earthly realm. In this sense, they help to bring Heaven to earth.

To the mystic, the spirit realm is a safe place. To them, the spiritual realm can often seem more real than the earthly realm. In fact, a mystic thrives on experiencing that heavenly realm.

(*The Happy Intercessor*, Chapter 11)

Define a mystic in your own words.

Research a Christian mystic on the Internet and absorb their story into your prayer life.

DAY 39

Mystics—Super and Natural

One thing I have desired of the Lord, that will I seek: that I may dwell in the house of the Lord all of the days of my life, to behold the beauty of the Lord and to inquire in His temple (Psalm 27:4).

DEVOTION

To me, the mystics are just normal people. They are normal people consumed by the presence of God. They are normal people who enjoy being with God and who know how to move in and out of the secret place.

I used to think of mystics as people who just stayed secluded with God and hid themselves away from other people and from the world. But many of the mystics did not stay secluded. In fact, a lot of them lived in the world and touched the world. Saints Patrick and Columba are examples of two mystics who chose to impact the world around them with the Kingdom of God. These two men were great evangelists who moved in signs and wonders. Although they lived for the heartbeat of Heaven, they also chose to bring the Kingdom of Heaven to the earth. They knew how to touch the Father's heart, yet they moved among the people and ministered. And a long time ago, I decided that, if they can do both, I can do both.

(*The Happy Intercessor*, Chapter 11)

REFLECTIONS

1. Did you define mystics as "normal people who enjoy being with God and who know how to move in and out of the secret place"?

2. Do you know of mystics who prefer to stay secluded?

3. Have you witnessed great evangelists who move in signs and wonders?

4. What does it mean to you to live for the heartbeat of Heaven?

5. If mystics can touch the Father's heart, yet move among the people and minister, can you too?

MEDITATIVE ACTION

Some people I would describe as modern-day mystics live extremely normal lives. Some of the most mystical people I know today are able to function in the world around them, even though they spend much of their time living in the spiritual realm. They get their life and their breath from the secret place. The most important thing to them is seeking the face of God, and they have a desire and a passion to know what God is doing and to hear what He is saying. They are desperate to hear the heartbeat of Heaven. Without that connection with Heaven, they begin to feel unbalanced.

A mystical person who is in a right relationship with God and humankind will naturally open the gates for other people to go to the same places in the spiritual realm that he or she has discovered.

(*The Happy Intercessor*, Chapter 11)

If you are a mystic, ask God to allow you to make yourself known to open the gates for other people to experience the spiritual realm.

If not a mystic, seek out a modern-day mystic or become familiar with one of the past to experience the spiritual realm as never before.

DAY 40

Meditate Within Your Heart

Be angry, and do not sin. Meditate within your heart on your bed, and be still. Selah (Psalm 4:4).

DEVOTION

By now you have figured out that having an intimate relationship with the Three-ness, the Holy Trinity, is vital in an intercessor's life. We must learn to know the Father, the Son, and the Holy Spirit. Being righteous is being in right standing with God, the Trinity. The Bible says that the effective, fervent prayers of a righteous person avails (profits) much (see James 5:16). The Message Bible says it this way: "The prayer of a person living right with God is something powerful to be reckoned with." We must have an ongoing relationship with the Trinity and be constant in our pursuit of this heavenly presence. We must experience the Godhead.

All of the words in this devotional come down to one thing: time spent with God. There is a place in all of us that cannot be filled with anything but God. It's a deep place for us to dwell with our heavenly Father. In order for us to get to this place, we must quiet ourselves inside and learn to know and feel Him.

(*The Happy Intercessor*, Chapter 11)

REFLECTIONS

1. How intimately do you know the Father, the Son, and the Holy Spirit?

2. Are you righteous, in right standing with God, the Trinity?

3. Do you have an ongoing relationship with the Trinity and are you constant in your pursuit of this heavenly presence?

4. Are you dwelling in the deep place with your heavenly Father?

5. Are you prepared to quiet yourself inside and learn to know and feel Him?

MEDITATIVE ACTION

Tonight, as you lay your head on your pillow, let all of the stuff from your day just fall off, and begin to think on Him. Meditate in your heart about His goodness. Read a verse or pick a word that describes Him and begin to connect your spirit with His. Take some time and practice being still before Him. Words won't be necessary. One of the proposed meanings of the word *selah* is "to pause and ponder." Ponder the things of God. As you practice this, you will soon be lost and caught up in His presence. You will begin to understand His world.

(*The Happy Intercessor*, Chapter 11)

Meditate within your heart on a Scripture verse that brings you close to Him.

Be still—and know that He is God.

APPENDIX:
A Big Dose of Joy

Joy means "a feeling of great happiness or pleasure, especially of an elevated or spiritual kind." There are other words that associate with the word *joy*: delight, happiness, pleasure, bliss, ecstasy, elation, and thrill. The word *ecstasy* means "a feeling of intense delight." The word *bliss* means "perfect untroubled happiness."

The word *joy* is in the Bible 182 times. I have picked out several references on joy for you to read. I feel that it is important to include these verses in this book. They are reminders to us of the importance of being a joyful people, of being who we were created to be. Not only that, but it is important that we as believers represent, or re-present, who our heavenly Father is here on earth. He is loving and joyful. He laughs from Heaven. Most of the verses have several translations for your enjoyment.

Psalm 21:6—*For You make him most blessed forever; You make him joyful with gladness in Your presence* (NASB).

Psalm 68:3—*But let the righteous be glad; let them exult before God; yes, let them rejoice with gladness* (NASB).

Psalm 100:2—*Serve the Lord with gladness; come before Him with joyful singing* (NASB).

Gladness is experiencing joy and pleasure. In these verses, we see that being in God's presence brings gladness.

Isaiah 55:12—*For you will go out with joy And be led forth with peace; the mountains and the hills will break forth into shouts of joy before you, and all the trees of the field will clap their hands* (NASB).

Isaiah 55:12—*For you shall go out with joy, and be led forth with peace: the mountains and the hills shall break forth before you into singing; and all the trees of the fields shall clap their hands* (WEB).

Isaiah 55:12—*For you shall go out in joy, and be led back in peace; the mountains and the hills before you shall burst into song, and all the trees of the field shall clap their hands* (NRSV).

Isaiah 55:12—*So you'll go out in joy, you'll be led into a whole and complete life. The mountains and hills will lead the parade, bursting with song. All the trees of the forest will join the procession, exuberant with applause* (TM).

Jeremiah 15:16—*Your words were found and I ate them, and Your words became for me a joy and the delight of my heart; for I have been called by Your name, O Lord God of hosts* (NASB).

Jeremiah 15:16—*Your words were found, and I ate them, and Your word was to me the joy and rejoicing of my heart; for I am called by Your name, O Lord God of hosts* (NKJV).

Jeremiah 15:16—*When your words showed up, I ate them—swallowed them whole. What a feast! What delight I took in being yours, O God, God of-the-Angel-Armies* (TM).

Zephaniah 3:17—*The Lord your God is in your midst, a victorious warrior. He will exult over you with joy, He will be quiet in His love, He will rejoice over you with shouts of joy* (NASB).

Zephaniah 3:17—*The Lord your God in your midst, the Mighty One, will save; He will rejoice over you with gladness, He will quiet you with His love, He will rejoice over you with singing* (NKJV).

Zephaniah 3:17—*The Lord, your God, is in your midst, a warrior who gives victory; He will rejoice over you with gladness, He will renew you in His love; He will exult over you with loud singing* (NRSV).

Zephaniah 3:17—*Your God is present among you, a strong Warrior there to save you. Happy to have you back, He'll calm you with His love and delight you with His songs* (TM).

Zechariah 8:19—*Thus says the Lord of hosts, "The fast of the fourth, the fast of the fifth, the fast of the seventh and the fast of the tenth months will become joy, gladness, and cheerful feasts for the house of Judah; so love truth and peace"* (NASB).

John 15:11—*These things I have spoken to you so that My joy may be in you, and that your joy may be made full* (NASB).

John 15:11—*I've told you these things for a purpose: that My joy might be your joy, and your joy wholly mature* (TM).

John 15:11—*I have said these things to you so that My joy may be in you, and that your joy may be complete* (NRSV).

John 15:11—*These things I have spoken to you, that My joy in you may remain, and your joy may be full* (YLT).[2]

John 15:11—*I have spoken these things to you that My joy may be in you, and your joy be full* (DRBY).[3]

John 17:13—*But now I come to You, and these things I speak in the world, that they may have My joy fulfilled in themselves* (NKJV).

John 17:13—*But now I come to You; and these things I speak in the world so that they may have My joy made full in themselves* (NASB).

John 17:13—*Now I'm returning to you. I'm saying these things in the world's hearing. So My people can experience My joy completed in them* (TM).

Acts 13:52—*And the disciples were continually filled with joy and with the Holy Spirit* (NASB).

Acts 13:52—*Brimming with joy and the Holy Spirit, two happy disciples* (TM).

Acts 13:52—*The disciples were filled with joy with the Holy Spirit* (WEB).

Acts 2:28—*You have made known to me the ways of life; You will make me full of gladness with Your presence* (NASB).

Acts 15:3—*Therefore, being sent on their way by the church, they were passing Through both Phoenicia and Samaria, describing in detail the conversion of the Gentiles, and were bringing great joy to all the brethren* (NASB).

Acts 15:3—*After they were sent off and on their way, they told everyone they met as they traveled through Phoenicia and Samaria about the breakthrough to the Gentile outsiders. Everyone who heard the news cheered—it was terrific news* (TM).

Acts 15:3—*They, being sent on their way by the assembly, passed through both Phoenicia and Samaria, declaring the conversion of the Gentiles. They caused great joy to all the brothers* (WEB).

Romans 14:17—*For the kingdom of God is not eating and drinking, but righteousness and peace and joy in the Holy Spirit* (NASB).

Romans 14:17—*For the kingdom of God is not eating and drinking, but righteousness, and peace, and joy in [the] Holy Spirit* (DRBY).

Romans 14:17—*God's kingdom isn't a matter of what you put in your stomach, for goodness' sake. It's what God does with your life as He sets it right, puts it together, and completes it with joy* (TM).

Romans 15:13—*Now may the God of hope fill you with all joy and peace in believing, so that you will abound in hope by the power of the Holy Spirit* (NASB).

Romans 15:13—Oh! May the God of green hope fill you up with joy, fill you up with peace, so that your believing lives, filled with the life-giving energy of the Holy Spirit, will brim over with hope (TM).

Romans 15:13—and the God of the hope shall fill you with all joy and peace in the believing, for your abounding in the hope in power of the Holy Spirit (YLT).

Psalms 51:12—Restore to me the joy of Your salvation and sustain me with a willing spirit (NASB).

Psalm 51:12—Restore unto me the joy of Thy salvation; and uphold me with a willing spirit (ASV).[4]

Psalm 51:12—Restore to me the joy of Thy salvation, and a willing spirit doth sustain me (YLT).

Psalm 51:12—Bring me back from gray exile, put a fresh wind in my sails (TM).

Psalm 16:11—You will make known to me the path of life; in Your presence is Fullness of joy; in Your right hand there are pleasures forever (NASB).

Psalm 16:11—Thou causest me to know the path of life; Fullness of joys [is] with Thy presence, pleasant things by Thy right hand forever! (YLT)

Psalm 16:11—Thou wilt make known to me the path of life: Thy countenance is fulness of joy; at thy right hand are pleasures for evermore (DRBY).

Nehemiah 8:10—Then he said to them, "Go, eat of the fat, drink of the sweet, and send portions to him who has nothing prepared; for this day is holy to our Lord. Do not be grieved, for the joy of the Lord is strength" (NASB).

Nehemiah 8:10—Then he said to them, "Go your way, eat the fat and drink sweet wine and send portions of them to those for whom nothing is prepared, for this day is holy to our Lord; and do not be grieved, for the joy of the Lord is your strength" (NRSV).

Nehemiah 8:10—*And he saith to them, "Go, eat fat things, and drink sweet things, and sent portions to him for whom nothing is prepared, for to-day* [is] *holy to our Lord, and be not grieved, for the joy of Jehovah is your strength"* (YLT).

Nehemiah 8:10—*He continued, "Go home and prepare a feast, holiday food and drink; and share it with those who don't have anything: This day is holy to God. Don't feel bad. The joy of God is your strength"* (TM).

1 Chronicles 16:27—*Splendor and majesty are before Him, strength and **joy** are in His place* (NASB).

1 Chronicles 16:27—*Splendor and majesty flow out of Him, strength and joy fill His place* (TM).

1 Chronicles 16:27—*Splendor and majesty are before Him; strength and joy in His dwelling place* (NIV).

1 Chronicles 16:27—*Honor and majesty are before Him: Strength and gladness are in His place* (ASV).

Matthew 25:21—*His master said to him, "Well done, good and faithful slave. You were faithful with a few things, I will put you in charge of many things; enter into the joy of your master"* (NASB).

Matthew 25:21—*His master replied, "Well done, good and faithful servant! You have been faithful with a few things; I will put you in charge of many things. Come and share your master's happiness"* (NIV).

Hebrews 12:2—*Let us fix our eyes on Jesus, the author and perfecter of our faith, who for the joy set before Him endured the cross, scorning its shame, and sat down at the right hand of the throne of God* (NIV).

Hebrews 12:2—*Looking steadfastly on Jesus the leader and completer of faith: who, in view of the joy lying before Him, endured* [the] *cross, having despised* [the] *shame, and is set down at the right hand of the throne of God* (DRBY).

Hebrews 12:2—*looking to the author and perfecter of faith—Jesus, who, over against the joy set before Him—did endure a cross, shame having despised, on the right hand also of the throne of God did sit down* (YLT).

Hebrews 12:2—*Looking to Jesus the pioneer and perfecter of our faith, who for the sake of the joy that was set before Him endured the cross...* (NKJV).

ENDNOTES

1. *The New Webster Encyclopedic Dictionary of the English Language*, s.v.v. "Joy," "Ecstasy," "Bliss."

2. YLT, Young's Literal Translation.

3. DRBY, Darby Translation.

4. ASV, American Standard Version.

Recommended Reading

A Life of Miracles by Bill Johnson

Basic Training for the Prophetic Ministry by Kris Vallotton

Basic Training for the Supernatural Ways of Royalty by Kris Vallotton

Developing a Supernatural Lifestyle by Kris Vallotton

Dreaming With God by Bill Johnson

Face to Face by Bill Johnson

Here Comes Heaven by Bill Johnson

Purity by Kris Vallotton

Strengthen Yourself in the Lord by Bill Johnson

The Supernatural Power of a Transformed Mind by Bill Johnson

The Supernatural Ways of Royalty by Bill Johnson and Kris Vallotton

The Ultimate Treasure Hunt by Kevin Dedmon

When Heaven Invades Earth by Bill Johnson

Author's Ministry
and Contact Information

www.bjm.org/beni

www.ibethel.org

To contact the author please visit:

www.benij.org

www.happyintercessor.com

www.ibethel.org

REFLECTIONS

REFLECTIONS

REFLECTIONS

REFLECTIONS

REFLECTIONS

REFLECTIONS

REFLECTIONS

REFLECTIONS

IN THE RIGHT HANDS, THIS BOOK WILL CHANGE LIVES!

Most of the people who need this message will not be looking for this book. To change their lives, you need to put a copy of this book in their hands.

> *But others (seeds) fell into good ground, and brought forth fruit, some a hundred-fold, some sixty-fold, some thirty-fold* (Matthew 13:8).

Our ministry is constantly seeking methods to find the good ground, the people who need this anointed message to change their lives. Will you help us reach these people?

> *Remember this—a farmer who plants only a few seeds will get a small crop. But the one who plants generously will get a generous crop* (2 Corinthians 9:6).

EXTEND THIS MINISTRY BY SOWING
3 BOOKS, 5 BOOKS, 10 BOOKS, OR MORE TODAY,
AND BECOME A LIFE CHANGER!

Thank you,

Don Nori Sr., Founder
Destiny Image
Since 1982

DESTINY IMAGE PUBLISHERS, INC.

"Promoting Inspired Lives."

VISIT OUR NEW SITE HOME AT
WWW.DESTINYIMAGE.COM

FREE SUBSCRIPTION TO DI NEWSLETTER

Receive free unpublished articles by top DI authors, exclusive
discounts, and free downloads from our best and newest books.
Visit www.destinyimage.com to subscribe.

Write to: Destiny Image
              P.O. Box 310
              Shippensburg, PA 17257-0310

Call: 1-800-722-6774

Email: orders@destinyimage.com

For a complete list of our titles or to place an order
online, visit www.destinyimage.com.

FIND US ON FACEBOOK OR FOLLOW US ON TWITTER.

www.facebook.com/destinyimage   **facebook**
www.twitter.com/destinyimage   **twitter**